A Revised and Expanded Edition of the Classic Best-seller

HELP I'M A PARENT

How to Handle Temper Tantrums, Sibling Fights, Questions About Sex, and Other Parenting Challenges

DR. BRUCE NARRAMORE

ZondervanPublishingHouse
Grand Rapids, Michigan

A Division of HarperCollinsPublishers

Help! I'm a Parent, Revised Edition
Copyright © 1995 by Bruce Narramore

Requests for information should be addressed to:
Zondervan Publishing House
Grand Rapids, Michigan 49530

Library of Congress Cataloging-in-Publication Data

Narramore, Bruce.
    Help! I'm a parent: how to handle temper tantrums, sibling fights, questions
about sex, and other parenting challenges / Bruce Narramore.— Rev. and
expanded ed.
        p.   cm.
    Includes bibliographical references and index.
    ISBN 0-310-46211-8 (soft.)
    1. Child psychology. 2. Child rearing. I. Title.
BF721.N33   1995
649'.1–dc20   94-37007
                                                                       CIP

Doonesbury cartoons copyright 1987 by G. B. Trudeau. Reprinted with permission
of Universal Press Syndicate. All rights reserved.

Calvin and Hobbes cartoons copyright by Watterson. Dist. by Universal Press
Syndicate. Reprinted with permission. All rights reserved.

McPherson cartoons copyright 1991 by John McPherson. All rights reserved.

Family Circus cartoons reprinted with special permission of King Features
Syndicate.

All Scripture quotations, unless otherwise indicated, are taken from the Holy Bible,
New International Version®. NIV®. Copyright © 1973, 1978, 1984 by International Bible Society. Used by permission of Zondervan Publishing House. All rights
reserved.

Edited by Rachel Boers
Interior design by Sue Koppenol

Printed in the United States of America

95 96 97 98 99 00 01 02 03/❖ DH/ 10 9 8 7 6 5 4 3 2

CONTENTS

Acknowledgments

Many people have contributed to this book. The willingness of thousands of parents to share their struggles with me and to search for workable solutions to problems in their families is the foundation without which the book could not have been written.

My wife, Kathy, played a key role in developing the book's first edition. We spent many hours discussing child-rearing practices and learning from our own successes and mistakes. As the manuscript was written, she moved between the roles of supportive, encouraging spouse and insightful, helpful critic.

Our children, Richard and Debbie, gave me a chance to "practice what I preach" and made parenting a wonderful, enriching experience. Now that they are young adults, they continue to help by being my friends and by sharing their experiences and perceptions with me. Richard, who is now a professional editor, gave up several lengthy weekends to read and edit this entire manuscript. I can't think of a greater privilege than having one of my grown children honestly reflect on my book on rearing children and give thoughtful, helpful (if sometimes painful!) feedback. If this book is clearer and more lively and well written than the first edition, Richard deserves most of the credit.

I also wish to express my appreciation to Jackie Haynes for her very helpful suggestions on working mothers, and for her editorial input. Jackie was also the one who told me, "You must use these Calvin and Hobbes cartoons!"

I owe a debt to each of these people and deeply appreciate their contributions to my life and to this second edition of *Help! I'm a Parent*.

CHAPTER 1

Help! I'm a Parent

After a tough day with two rambunctious preschoolers, a weary mother declared, "From the minute I got up this morning my kids were fussing and fighting and finding creative ways to drive me nuts. I tried everything to get them to settle down, but nothing worked. Sometimes on a day like this I just want to give them away cheap!" After a similar day with two teenagers, another frazzled mother confided, "I love them to death, but some days I'd like to knock them into the middle of next week!"

If you have children you know how these mothers feel. Parenting can be a wonderful, enriching experience, but it isn't always a piece of cake. Humorist Dave Barry clipped an article from the American Medical Association newsletter about a man who went to his doctor complaining of a hearing loss. When the doctor checked it out, he found that the man's ear canal was blocked by a plug of hardened superglue! Barry comments:

> Now some of you are scratching your heads and wondering, "how does a person with an IQ higher than pastry get superglue in his *ear* and not know it?" but you parents out there are no doubt nodding your heads and saying: "It would not surprise me to learn that this man has a three-year-old son."
>
> And, of course you're right. According to the AMA newsletter, the son "squirted the glue into the father's left ear when the man was sleeping." Fortunately surgeons were able to unclog the man's ear, but as medical consumers we can prevent this kind of ear-tragedy by remembering to take these safety precautions:

1. Never keep three-year-old children around the house.
2. If you do, never sleep.[1]

Your children may not be quite so creative as to put superglue in your ear, but I'm sure they create their share of problems. If you have a toddler, you are probably facing meal or bedtime hassles, problems with toilet training, temper tantrums, and whining. If you have preschoolers, they have probably added fighting, talking back, and sibling rivalry to your life. Elementary school children are good at creating messy rooms and homework hassles, and squabbling with their friends. They also forget their chores, crouch outside their sister's room like a cat outside a mouse hole, and are melodramatically bored on rainy days!

Eleven- and twelve-year-olds are approaching adolescence at the speed of light and will soon acquire some dubious friends, clothes, music, grades, or attitudes. And if you have a fifteen- or sixteen-year-old, you are no doubt encountering occasional negativism, hypersensitivity, moodiness, and worries about their friends and the opposite sex.

If these problems only popped up say, once or twice a month, most of us could cope just fine. But when they pile on top of each other for sixteen hours a day, or when you are trying to hold down a job and rear children at the same time, they quickly press us to the borders of our parental patience—if not our sanity! As another mother of preschoolers told me, "It's amazing how two small children with half my intelligence can make me feel so helpless and infuriated."

This book shows you how to manage your children so that you avoid or solve most of these hassles. I'm convinced that you don't need to spend your whole day solving problems, refereeing fights, picking up after your children, and reminding them to put on their coats or to study for tomorrow's math quiz. You can even teach your children to get along with each other—most of the time!

Unfortunately, newborn babies don't come equipped with an owner's manual telling us how to solve these problems. So we do what comes naturally: We coax, plead, bribe, nag, threaten, and punish. Or we reach into our memory banks for the techniques our parents used on us. But while those old methods provide temporary relief, it doesn't last long, and they miss the more important emotional and relational issues behind your children's exasperating behaviors. This book gives you something like an owner's manual for children from the toddler stage through the middle teens. By the time you finish you will know:

- What causes your children to misbehave and how to head off many of their misbehaviors before they get out of control
- How you may be unconsciously training your children to do the very things you hate
- How to increase your children's positive, cooperative, and likeable behaviors
- Six easy, practical techniques of discipline that will show positive results in your family within a week
- How to get your children to clean their rooms and do their chores without constantly nagging and reminding them
- How to handle your children's two biggest excuses—"I couldn't hear you" and "I forgot"
- How to help your children feel better about themselves and about you so they won't misbehave out of frustration

NO PH.D.'S FOR PARENTS

Our society requires seventeen years of education before certifying a person to teach in public school. Medical doctors and psychologists must have twenty years of schooling before they practice on your children. And many states require teenagers to take a course in driver's education before they can be licensed to drive a car. *But to rear children from the cradle to their twenties, our society doesn't require one hour of formal training!* Perhaps because conception, pregnancy, and childbirth are natural biological functions, we assume (if we think about it at all) that rearing children "just comes naturally." But it doesn't take long after the first baby arrives to realize that idea is incorrect. Most of us don't have the foggiest notion of how to see to it that our children eat their vegetables, let alone how to get them to clean their rooms, complete their chores, and live in relative peace around the home.

My wife and I were both college graduates and I had a Ph.D. before our children were born. We naively assumed we were ready for parenthood. But when Richard and Debbie arrived, we were rudely awakened. Even my four years of professional experience in child-guidance clinics and in public schools had not prepared me to cope with the daily routine of parenting. I had been trained to work with clinical problems like learning disorders, antisocial behavior, depression, and social withdrawal. But I hadn't learned how to get children to the dinner table, how to get them to behave in public, how to get them into bed, how to get them to do their homework, or how to keep them from killing each other!

Profound psychological labels I learned in graduate school such as "anxiety disorder of childhood" and "reactive attachment disorder" didn't really describe the problems I was facing. And even if they did, so what? We needed specific, practical advice on how to handle the daily behavior problems we were facing, not a bunch of psychological theory.

In addition to handling daily parenting chores, Kathy and I wanted to raise our children to love God and get along well with others. We knew that many spiritual and emotional problems have their roots in childhood traumas, and we wanted to spare Richard and Debbie as many of those problems as possible. So we started our own cram course in parenting. I read most of the popular books on child rearing and reviewed several of my graduate textbooks. I studied what the Bible has to say about parenting. I remembered my own childhood. And I tried to listen to what Richard and Debbie were telling me about why they were acting the way they did and how they were feeling.

That was twenty-five years ago. My wife and I and our children have all survived, and Richard and Debbie have grown up to be healthy and happy young adults. We even made it through adolescence! As I talk to parents today, however, I realize that it's even tougher rearing children than it was twenty years ago. Fewer than half of the children in America will be reared in a traditional intact family with their biological father and mother. Most will grow up with single parents or in blended families. As good as many of these families are, they still pose special struggles for parents and children. It's not easy coping with the loss of your mother or father or adapting to a stepparent or stepbrothers and stepsisters. And it is not easy parenting children who are trying to cope with these traumatic losses and changes at the same time you are struggling to adjust to a new mate or to being single.

Social and economic changes create other stresses. So many mothers work outside the home that parents have less time for their children. One study found that today's parents spend an average of ten to twelve fewer hours per week with their children than parents did in 1960. Another study found that one out of five teenagers had not had a ten-minute conversation with a parent in the past month![2] And nearly half of the mothers of children under three are working, most of them full-time.

Changing morals also make our job as parents tougher. In most high schools, it's no longer considered a virtue to be a virgin. According to the National Center for Disease Control, forty percent of ninth graders in America (thirteen- and fourteen-year-olds) have had sexual intercourse! Three thousand teenage girls become pregnant in the United States every day. On top of that, one in every five teenagers is a problem drinker. Eroding morals and cultural values put incredible pressure on our children and make good training in the early years even more important.

EARTHLY FATHER, HEAVENLY FATHER

We all want well-behaved, happy children. But Christian parents also want to insure their children's moral and spiritual development. Your children's first concept of what God is like will come from you. Since God is a spiritual being in a seemingly distant heaven, your children have a difficult time comprehending who he is. All children are like the young boy who was afraid to sleep alone in his room at night. When his father assured him that God was there and would protect him, the little boy replied, "But I need somebody with skin on him." Foreseeing this problem, God created you to be an earthly model of himself "with skin on." As your children grow up they will experience your protection, love, and discipline and their unconscious reasoning will go like this: "I have not seen God, my heavenly Father, but he must be like my earthly father and mother. Now I know what God is like." Despite all our human faults, children look at us to learn what God is like.

I once asked a woman I was counseling to describe her father. She replied, "He is honest, kind, just, and strong . . . but he is so busy I hardly know him." Some weeks later I asked her to tell me about her view of God. She replied, "He is loving, kind, just, and omnipotent . . . but he seems so distant I hardly know him." She used almost the exact words to describe God and her own father! This is common.

Think of your own experience. Haven't you ever been afraid God didn't understand you or was going to get even with you? Haven't you occasionally had difficulty believing God's will was best for you? Haven't you ever felt God was far away or uninterested in you? Or haven't you wondered if God is really fair and loving? Most of these feelings are at least partially the result of emotional hangovers from childhood experiences with our parents.

Jesus used this parallel between earthly parent and heavenly Father when he said, "If you, then, though you are evil, know how to give good gifts to your children, how much more will your Father in heaven give good gifts to those who ask him!"[3]

This puts child rearing in an entirely different light. As you train and discipline your children you aren't just solving problems, teaching them to be responsible, or getting a little peace and quiet around the house. You are actually influencing their attitudes toward God! If your children feel loved by you they will find it easier to understand God's love and care. If they experience you as emotionally distant, punitive, or controlling they will tend to see God the same way. Your parenting has spiritual and eternal effects on your children.

A SHORT COURSE IN PARENTING

In the following pages I will show how you can handle the bothersome everyday problems children get into, and how to nourish their emotional and spiritual needs at the same time. In the next two chapters we will see what causes children to misbehave. Then I will show you a biblical pattern of parenting that uses God's relationship with us as a model for disciplining our children. Chapters 5 through 9 describe six techniques of discipline and apply them to everyday problems like preventing sibling squabbles, handling temper tantrums, and getting children to do their chores and homework without a thousand reminders. Chapters 10 through 13 discuss four especially important areas of parenting—your child's self-esteem, sex education, working mothers, and how to cope with your angry feelings in ways that won't damage your children. Chapter 15 looks at several of the most frequent questions parents ask, like, "How can I handle a child who keeps waking up and crying in the middle of the night?" "What should I do when my children act up in public?" and "How can I get my children to stop fighting?" The book closes with a chapter on how to keep on growing as a parent.

Before we go further, however, I want to encourage you. A lot of child-rearing authorities are down on parents. They imply that a few simple mistakes will ruin your children for life. That simply is not true. Children are amazingly resilient. They don't need perfect parents; they need parents who are sensitive and kind most of the time—but children *can* handle occasional misunderstandings and anger and frustration, as long as that's not the steady diet. When your children push you to your limits and you say or do things you regret, don't get too bent out of shape. Just step back and give yourself time to cool off. Talk the situation over with your spouse or a friend until you get things into perspective. Then apologize to your children and move ahead. If you blame yourself for every failure or misunderstanding, you will become so tense and feel so guilty that you won't be able to enjoy your children and give them what they really need—a generally happy and enjoyable relationship with their mom and dad.

If you are a single parent, the same applies to you. Of course it's more difficult rearing children alone, and you won't be able to give them everything you could if you had a spouse. But you can still be an excellent parent. In fact, one healthy parent can do a better job than two fighting, unhappy parents. In chapter 13 I will offer some special suggestions for solo parents and working mothers, but for now let me encourage you: You can make it. A lot of very healthy, happy kids have been reared by single parents!

Notes

1. Dave Barry, *Dave Barry Talks Back* (New York: Crown, 1991), 62–63.
2. Nina Easton, "Every place, enemies of the family," *L A Times*, 1 March 1992.
3. Matthew 7:11.

CHAPTER 2

Children Misbehave When Their Needs Aren't Met

Think back to a particularly bad day with your children. Shortly after you climbed out of bed—maybe while you were still asleep—things started going wrong. Your youngest child crashed to the floor in another room of the house. Your oldest child was ready to kill because her new white Reeboks had been decorated by her brother with his fire-engine-red crayon. From that beginning things got even worse. By the end of the day, you were asking yourself, "What did I do to deserve this?" or "What in the world is the matter with these kids?" In fact, you may have decided that no two or three normal children could cause that much trouble unless they stayed up late the night before plotting the whole thing!

If you are going to keep your sanity, you have to understand what causes children to create those hectic days. In this chapter and in chapter 3 we will look at the nine main reasons children misbehave. We are starting with the reasons children misbehave because knowing the reason is the first step in changing things. Just like you can't get your stalled car running until you know whether the problem is a dead battery or a ruined transmission, you can't get your children to clean up their rooms or do their homework or get along with each other until you learn why they *aren't* doing those things.

THE SEARCH FOR ATTENTION

Have you ever been in the kitchen preparing dinner when your daughter walked in and asked, "Mommy, will you play with me?" If you were busy you probably told her, "I'm sorry, honey. Mommy is busy right now." She turned away and went off to play but returned a few minutes later. With increasing intensity in her voice she asked, "*Mommy*, will you play with me *now*?" And with growing frustration in your voice, you replied, "*Honey*, can't you see I'm busy? I can't play now!" Then she dropped her head and trudged off to the other end of the house.

A half hour later you suddenly realized she had been too quiet for too long, so you went back to investigate. You found the first clues in the hallway: a glob of shaving cream on the rug and an incriminating trail of baby powder. You followed the trail into your bedroom and—behold!—your daughter had created a mural on your wall with nail polish. Your room was enhanced with the smell of perfume, and extravagant toilet-paper decorations draped your lamp, vanity, and bathroom.

This scene, played out in millions of homes, introduces the first six reasons children misbehave. Children have four basic God-given emotional needs. They are:

- The need to feel loved
- The need to feel confident
- The need to feel significant and worthwhile
- The need to be involved in interesting, constructive activities

When these needs are met, children feel good about themselves and get into a minimum of mischief. When these needs aren't met (and they cannot always be), children feel badly, so they start looking for substitutes for their God-given needs. Unfortunately, to find those substitutes they misbehave. When your daughter turned into a mischievous Michelangelo, for example, she probably felt temporarily neglected, ignored, or unloved. She compensated for those feelings by doing something she knew would gain your attention. Her actions said, "Mom, if you won't spend time with me and show me you love me when I am behaving well, I know that if I get into trouble you will give me a little attention." Someone has said, "For every God-given need, Satan has a substitute." This is certainly true in the emotional arena. *Love is the first God-given need*, and any kind of attention—even negative—becomes the substitute for a deep feeling of belonging or being loved.

Children Misbehave When Their Needs Aren't Met

We adults aren't any different from our children. When we feel our spouse or a friend is ignoring us, we may give them a direct message like "I need some time with you" or "I'm feeling less important to you than your work." But if that doesn't work we start picking fights or causing other problems, because we know that once we upset them enough they will give us some attention. If *we* do that, think how much more likely our children are to resort to the same tactic.

Children who feel unloved or left out even risk punishment because it temporarily reassures them that they matter. They write on walls, start battles with their brother or sister, interrupt us, under-achieve at school, or engage in delinquent behavior, because they know we will at least give them attention when we spank them, tell them to "shape up," complain about their grades, or bail them out of jail.

There are three steps in this attention-getting cycle. First, children feel unloved or left out. Next, they feel bad because they don't feel loved. Finally, they misbehave in order to temporarily feel better by gaining attention.

Unmet need for love	→	Painful emotions of loneliness and sadness	→	Misbehavior designed to gain attention

More childhood misbehavior is caused by this misguided search for attention than any other single thing. That's because most American parents are so busy that we don't take enough concentrated time to be with our children. As one father put it, "I can *support* my family or I can be *with* my family, but I can't do both." Even when we are in the same room, we can be so preoccupied with our own activities that we aren't emotionally present. And the moment children feel left out, they start interrupting, fighting, fussing, breaking things, or crying in order to get our attention. Teenagers dress in outrageous ways, become sexually promiscuous, take dangerous risks, develop an exaggerated social life with the popular crowd, or become the class clown in order to get attention.

I am not saying that you don't love your children if they are engaging in some of these attention-getting behaviors. I am sure you do. But at the moment they turn to these attention-getting devices, they aren't *feeling* loved or included. Young children, especially, have small emotional fuel tanks that need to be refueled every few minutes with a hug or words of encouragement. Older children can go longer without refueling, but they still need frequent "emotional fill-ups."

If you want to keep your children out of trouble, you will have to anticipate the times they will feel lonely, neglected, or left out, and then do your best to spend time with them before the painful feelings get out of hand. Can your two-year-old daughter go thirty minutes without a tangible sign of your love? An hour? Half a day? Two- and three-year-olds have very short attention spans and need constant reminders of our love and care. As she grows older, she will be able to entertain herself and be alone for longer periods without feeling unloved. But even teenagers need some time every day to touch base with Mom and Dad.

"TWO OR THREE MONTHS AGO I WAS ALWAYS EXHAUSTED BECAUSE HE NEEDED CONSTANT ATTENTION. NOW THAT HE'S ABLE TO ENTERTAIN HIMSELF, LIFE IS SO MUCH EASIER."

You can show your love for young children by being sure they aren't left alone for long stretches of time, and by setting aside regular times to talk, play, or work together. It is also a good idea to occasionally stop what you are doing to give them a hug and let them know you will be with them as soon as you finish. You can show your love for older children and teenagers by being available when they come home from school, listening to them talk about their day's activities, and taking an interest in their friends. Shopping, repairing the car, and attending their soccer games or drill team performances are great activities to do together.

THE SEARCH FOR POWER OR CONTROL

Do you remember the look of glee in your year-old daughter's eyes the first time she toddled across the living room under her own power? She was thrilled because she finally realized, "I can do it! I'm not a helpless baby anymore!" And do you remember that strong, stubborn look on your two-year-old's face as he firmly announced, "No! I won't!"? He was giving you the same message! Two years ago he didn't exist. A year ago he was a helpless baby living in a world of seemingly all-powerful giants. But now he is finding out that he can influence the world, or at least he can say no to a huge parent, which to him is just as good. If you are two years old, the power to say no when your parent issues a command is a great achievement. It is like a junior higher being negativistic or a teenager wearing a weird hairdo. It says, "I'm not a baby anymore. I'm my own person. I can do things *my* way."

Your toddler's excitement and your two-year-old's stubborn "no" reflect their success in meeting their next God-given need—to feel confident. Infants are totally dependent. Soon they find out that when they cry, someone comes and cares for them. As they grow, they gradually learn to do things for themselves. They walk and talk. They tie their shoes, and eventually they write their names. Each small achievement builds their budding confidence and prepares them for the time they will have to get a job, buy a house, or get along with others outside the home.

Children who fail to develop confidence feel anxious and inferior. Since those are painful feelings, they look for a substitute for the God-given need for confidence. That substitute is power, stubbornness, or control of others. Children who lack confidence either give up and become shy and withdrawn, or they become stubborn and controlling. Some turn into bullies or little tyrants who refuse to cooperate, or who put down their siblings in order to repress their feelings of helplessness. By making others feel small, they feel big. This cycle works just like the attention cycle.

Unmet need	→	Painful emotions	→	Misbehavior
for confidence		of weakness,		designed
		inferiority,		to make the child
		and anxiety		feel powerful

Unfortunately, the false confidence that comes from stubbornness and control is like alcohol. It temporarily numbs the pain, but does nothing to cure the real problem. Deep down, these children still feel weak and inferior, because no human being can ever feel truly good about himself when he builds that feeling on mistreatment of others.

The only sure way to help your children avoid this stubborn pitfall—or grow out of it if they have already fallen into it—is to help them feel better about themselves. When your daughter excitedly runs into the house yelling, "Mother, see what I made at school today?" she is looking to you to affirm her and build up her confidence. When your son says, "See how strong I am?" as he struggles into the house with a watermelon half his size, he is looking to you to admire him on work well done. Encourage your children. Give them small jobs at which they can succeed. Help them learn a sport or a skill, and don't criticize or compare them to other children. Each success builds up your children's confidence. Next to feeling loved, your children's *ability to function confidently and competently* is their most important emotional need. When it isn't met, it is the second most common cause of misbehavior.

THE SEARCH FOR PERFECTION

The mother of a newly adopted four-year-old girl told me how she disciplined her daughter. She said, "I was having a terrible time making my daughter behave until I finally told her, 'God doesn't love you when you're naughty!'"

I was stung by the fear and guilt this threat could instill in the little girl, so I asked, "Does God love *you* when *you* are naughty?" A sad but insightful look came over her face as she realized she had been manipulating her daughter by implying she was such a worthless and naughty person that God couldn't love her until she shaped up.

This mother was unknowingly violating her daughter's third deep emotional need—*the need to feel valuable, worthwhile, or significant.* The need to feel worthwhile is related to the need to feel confident, but is slightly different. A confident child knows she can perform well. A child with a sense of self-worth knows she is a valuable or significant person, instead of a bad or worthless one. When children lack a sense of confidence, they feel inferior or anxious. When they lack a sense of worth, they feel insignificant, bad, or guilty.

Like children who feel unloved or lack confidence, children with a deficient sense of worth either succumb to that painful feeling or try to find a substitute for their God-given need. Children who give in to feelings of worthlessness either become depressed and guilt-ridden, or decide to live up to their parents' lousy expectations by failing or becoming rebellious or disobedient. Children who try to fight off feelings of worthlessness turn to the substitute of perfectionism or performance.

Perfectionistic children try too hard to please. They strive for excellent grades or become excessively obedient and polite. But no matter how well they perform, or how good others think they are, they live with the nagging belief that they can never be quite good enough. Even well-behaved, straight-A students may be unable to convince themselves they really are worthwhile. The sad result is that even at the height of their success, when others are praising them, they remain fundamentally unhappy.

These children need a lot of help to learn to enjoy life and accept themselves the way they are. Otherwise they will enter adulthood with negative attitudes toward themselves, and will have great difficulty enjoying their lives, their families, and their successes.

Children develop a sense of significance and worth when they are listened to, when their feelings and opinions are taken seriously, and when they are spoken to respectfully. They also feel good about themselves when they are disciplined firmly, but lovingly. But their sense of worth is undermined when they are ignored, condemned, accused, or punished in anger. Here's the way the perfectionistic cycle works:

23

Unmet need to feel worthwhile	→	Painful feelings of depression, worthlessness, and guilt	→	Driven perfectionism or pressured performance

THE SEARCH FOR DESTRUCTIVE ACTIVITIES

Another need your children have is to participate in enjoyable and constructive activities. Children are naturally energetic and inquisitive, so if you don't keep them busy they quickly become bored. Children have special problems on rainy days when they can't go out to play, when they are cooped up in the backseat of the family car, or when they are trying to sit still in a long church service or at a fancy restaurant.

When my own children were young, the mere act of putting them in the backseat of the car set them fighting. Richard complained, "I want to sit there." Debbie yelled, "That's my side" or "He crossed the line!" (referring to the imaginary line dividing the backseat). Even though we eventually found a way to teach Richard and Debbie to get along, I didn't fully understand why they were fighting until several years later, when I was riding in the backseat with Debbie during an hour-long car trip in Australia. Our host picked up my wife, daughter, and me at the airport. Kathy climbed into the front seat, and I got into the backseat with Debbie. Before long, Kathy and our host started a serious conversation. After ten or fifteen miles, I grew bored. I reached over and gave Debbie a hug. She hugged me back. So far, so good. Then I gave her a little nudge on the ribs. Debbie nudged me back. Then I poked her a little harder. She poked me back, and soon we were hitting each other. Suddenly I wasn't bored or left out anymore. Debbie and I were having a great time fighting! Just as things were about to get out of hand I realized what was going on. I stopped and said, "Debbie, fighting is fun, isn't it?" With a look that asked where I had been all these years, Debbie replied, "Of course, Dad!"

That "fight" brought something to life that all of us have heard from our grandmothers: "Idle hands are the devil's workshop." Children need to be involved with constructive activities, or they will seek out destructive activities. *The attempt to overcome boredom* is the fourth reason children misbehave. What better way is there to bring some excitement into your life than starting a fight with your brother or getting into some kind of mischief? And it's a double "blessing" if you get some parental attention in the process!

Unmet need	→	Painful emotions	→	Search for
for constructive		of boredom		destructive
activity				activities

If you want to eliminate fighting and mischievous behavior, especially on long trips, rainy days, and holidays, you had better take time to plan some interesting activities to keep your children busy. A movie, a friend, an interesting game, or a great book can save you a lot of grief. Just yesterday, I asked a mother of five how she kept her sanity on long drives across the country in their family car. "It's easy," she replied. "We pack plenty of food and games and make frequent potty stops. And when we stop, I tell the kids, 'Go run up that hill as fast as you can.' When they get back, they are ready to sit down and travel." This mother won't need a child psychologist. She is one!

Table 1 (below) summarizes the first four reasons children misbehave. They all begin with a God-given emotional need that isn't fully met, and end up with problem behaviors that are designed to cover up painful feelings by finding substitutes for those God-given needs.

Table 1
NEEDS AND SUBSTITUTES

God-given Emotional Needs	*Painful Feelings When Need Isn't Met*	*Substitute Goals*
Love	Loneliness, Isolation, or Depression	Attention
Confidence	Inferiority, Anxiety	Power and Control
Worth	Worthlessness, Guilt, Depression	Perfectionism
Constructive Activity	Boredom	Destructive Activity

WARNING SIGNALS

Now that you see how this cycle works, you can understand one of the most important truths about children. Getting into trouble is often their way of trying to fulfill some God-given need. Misbehaving is our children's way of telling us, "Mom or Dad, right now I'm feeling unloved, incompetent, worthless, or bored." Instead of jumping on them for misbehaving, we need to see their misbehaviors as a cry for help. Once we help them meet their needs, they will be happier and better behaved.

This cycle also shows why it is so important to meet your children's needs *before* they misbehave. You can either take a little time planning your children's days and seeing that their needs are met, or you can spend a lot of time correcting and disciplining after they have gotten into trouble. In parenting it is really true that "an ounce of prevention is worth a pound of cure."

REVENGE AND SAFETY

Since your children's searches for attention, power, perfectionism, and destructive activities never solve the real problem, they will fall back on one of two other coping strategies. They will either *seek revenge on the people they are angry with for not meeting their needs, or they will try to find some psychological safety by erecting emotional barriers to keep people out and protect themselves from further hurt.*

Remember the adoptive mother who told her daughter, "God doesn't love you when you are naughty"? She was unknowingly destroying her daughter's feelings of significance and worth. Unless the mother changes, that girl will become discouraged and angry because her mom makes her feel so worthless. One of her best ways of retaliating against her mother's condemnations will be to become the "bad" child her mother claims she is. When this girl reaches adolescence she is likely to develop serious behavior problems in order to get even with her mother. Her behavior will say, "You think I'm worthless, so I'll show you just how worthless I can be!" Her mother can avoid this tragic chain of events by encouraging her daughter and avoiding guilt and shame-inducing accusations.

The rebellious son of a too-busy minister found a similar way to get revenge on his father for neglecting him. The boy told me, "I started drinking beer at fourteen, and when I was really drunk, I picked up a beer and said, 'Here's one for the deacons' board!'"

Other children get revenge on their parents or others by breaking things, getting poor grades, forgetting chores, or running away to get married. Sometimes the revenge is obvious, like picking on a new baby brother or sister. Other times the revenge is subtle—like children who do poorly in school to get even with parents who perpetually pressure them. But whether obvious or subtle, many children are nearly destroying themselves to get even with parents whom they feel do not love them, show enough confidence in them, or help them feel worthwhile.

When revenge doesn't silence the pain of unmet needs, children have only one remaining option: They have to find some way to block painful emotions out of their lives. I call this the search for psychological safety. Some children just stop feeling. They develop almost computer-like personalities to avoid experiencing any kind of emotion. They unconsciously say to themselves, "Since I have so many painful feelings, I will be better off if I just don't feel at all. I may miss some happy feelings, but at least I won't feel any sad ones."

Other children withdraw from social contact. They reason, "If I try to be accepted by my peers and they reject me it will be too painful, so I just won't try." Still others give up learning at school or competing in games and other activities. A girl whose confidence has been torn down by constant criticism may quit trying out for school plays or quit trying to please her parents. She thinks, "I can't do it anyway, so why try? If I don't try, I can't fail." This defeatist attitude is the saddest of all solutions. At least misbehaving children and children who are trying to get revenge are still fighting and attempting to meet their needs. Defeated children have given up entirely. Children like this need professional help to find out what went wrong so they can regain hope. They need to learn that they are loved, that they have abilities, and that they are valuable, significant individuals.

RECAP

Before we can discipline our children effectively, we need to know why they are misbehaving. In this chapter we looked at six reasons children misbehave.

- They are searching for attention because they are temporarily feeling unloved or left out.
- They are trying to gain power or control because they lack confidence and feel weak and helpless.
- They are trying to be perfect because they feel unworthy or bad about themselves.
- They are turning to some exciting but destructive activity because they are bored.
- They are trying to gain revenge or get even with those who have made them feel unloved, incompetent, unworthy, or bored.
- They are trying to find emotional safety and avoid bad feelings because they have given up hope.

In the next chapter we will look at the three other main reasons children misbehave.

CHAPTER 3

Kids Will Be Kids

From the day my wife and I brought our children home from the hospital, Richard and Debbie had different temperaments. Debbie had a hearty appetite, slept well, and was a contented baby. She was a happy, outgoing, adaptable child. Richard was another story. He was a great child, but from his earliest days he had a hard time getting to sleep at night, was a finicky eater, more inquisitive than Debbie, and a little shy. As they grew, Richard and Debbie were both affectionate, wonderful children, but they did not deviate significantly from their inborn, distinctly different temperaments. Richard was more strong-willed and difficult to discipline. Debbie rarely argued or lost her agreeable, flexible nature. Debbie was like her mother. Richard was like his dad.

Nowhere did these inborn differences show up more than in their attitudes toward neatness. From the time she was a very little girl, Debbie got up early, made her bed, and neatly arranged each of her dolls and stuffed animals in their proper places before Kathy and I even entered her room. When Kathy and I entertained, Debbie offered to help set the table, serve, and clean up afterward. Even when I cooked and left the kitchen in chaos, Debbie would come in and help with the cleanup. Richard wasn't afflicted with such a penchant for neatness. He would sleep in late, leaving his clothes, papers, and athletic equipment spread all over his room just like a normal boy. In fact, his room looked very much like his father's study!

Recently, Debbie and I were talking about her neatness. Since Kathy and I didn't have to train her to be that way, I wondered where it came from. I said, "Debbie, you have always been so neat and help-ful around the house. Why do you think that is?"

"I like to clean up," she replied.

I was shocked that any human being would actually enjoy cleaning up, so I said, "You must mean that you like things neat and clean. You don't actually enjoy cleaning up do you?"

"Yes," Debbie answered, "I like things neat, but I also enjoy cleaning up."

Isn't that incredible—a child who enjoys cleaning up? I wish I could tell you we taught that to Debbie, but we didn't. She came out of the womb that way!

Richard and Debbie demonstrate our next reason children act the way they do: Children come into this world with a tendency to react in different ways. They have different temperaments.[1] Some children are naturally easygoing. Others are upset by the slightest change in their routine. Some are morning people; others are night people. Some are energetic; others are lethargic. Some are easy to rear; some are difficult to manage. And all this happens before we parents even have a chance to mess them up. They are just born that way.

TEMPERAMENT AND MISBEHAVIOR

Inborn temperaments aren't really misbehaviors. There is nothing wrong with being quiet or active, outgoing or shy, inquisi-tive or easily satisfied. But these temperaments program our children to behave in ways that can become problematic. Take Timmy, for example. He was a persistent little four-year-old whose father com-plained that his son was "purposely" trying to upset him. He told me, "Timmy keeps asking questions like, 'Why is the sky blue?' 'What makes the stars shine?' and 'Why is grass green?' When I tell him, 'I don't know,' he just asks some more unanswerable questions. He won't quit until I finally just tell him to shut up."

As we talked, it became clear that Timmy wasn't purposely try-ing to upset this father. He was only trying to satisfy his curiosity—and perhaps gain his dad's attention. But since his dad didn't realize *why* Timmy was asking question after question, he was getting angrier and angrier at his son.

When his dad got angry, Timmy had two choices. He could keep quiet and squelch his God-given desires to understand the world and be with his dad, or he could ask more questions in order to get some answers and his father's attention. Timmy chose the latter. But the more questions he asked the more upset his dad became until finally Timmy got the attention he wanted—even if it wasn't the kind he was initially looking for.

Once Timmy's dad understood that his son's persistent questions grew out of a normal desire to be with his dad and understand his world, he was able to be more helpful. The next time Timmy asked a question he couldn't answer, his dad told him, "That's a great question, Son. I don't know the answer myself. Maybe you will learn that when you get in school." Another time when Timmy was in his inquisitive mode his dad simply told him, "You sure have a lot of questions today. I don't know the answers to most of them, but would you like to spend some time with Dad? We could go down to the library and check out some books or get an ice cream cone." And another time he told his son, "I wish I could answer your question but I have to do some of my own work now. I can be with you in an hour." Then he gave his son a hug and went on with his own activities.

These simple changes helped Timmy feel understood and important to his dad. They also relieved Timmy's dad, because he realized he had a normal, inquisitive child on his hands instead of a bothersome brat. If you have an energetic, inquisitive child like Timmy, or a child who can't sit still in church or in the car, he's probably not trying to make everyone around him miserable. Chances are he was born that way. The same is true if you have a slow child who has a hard time getting started in the morning, a finicky child who picks at her food for hours, a sensitive child whose feelings are easily hurt, a rambunctious child who is always pushing the limits, or a shy child who loves books but doesn't want to talk a lot or meet strangers. These children may all need help so their personality styles don't create problems. But these different styles are the source of their distinctive personalities. Rather than try to change their styles we need to help our children turn them into assets instead of liabilities.

NORMAL KIDS MISBEHAVE TOO

When our children were preschoolers, my wife occasionally led a Wednesday morning mothers' club. Kathy and several other mothers met to discuss how they could handle problems they were facing with their young children. One morning, the mother of three exclaimed, "I got so mad at my son this week I told him he was acting just like a two-year-old." When my wife asked, "How old *is* your son?" the mom hesitated and with an embarrassed look answered, "Two!"

"ALL RIGHT NOW, GIVE MOMMY THE SUPER GLUE."

There is a lesson here for every parent. Many of our children's misbehaviors are completely normal for their age. In fact, they may not even be misbehaviors at all. They may just be behaviors that bother us. Infants, for example, are supposed to cry. Since they can't talk, crying is the only way they can communicate. Toddlers are supposed to get messy and dirty. That's their job in life! Two-year-olds are supposed to say no. They are learning to think for themselves. Four- and five-year-olds are supposed to pester adults with a lot of questions. They want to know how this world works. Ten-year-old boys (and maybe girls, too) aren't supposed to desire a clean, neat room. Junior highers are supposed to be a little argumentative. Teenage girls are supposed to be moody and a little boy-crazy. And teenage boys are supposed to go through a negative, competitive period with their mom or dad.

Children who do these things—as long as they don't get completely carried away—are just going through some normal stages. They may need training or discipline, but you shouldn't jump to the conclusion that every time they act in these upsetting ways they are suffering from some deep emotional need you have been unable to satisfy.

One of my students recently brought me a poem that expresses this dilemma from a child's point of view.

God gave us fingers—Ma says, "Use your fork."
God gave us voices—Ma says, "Don't scream."
Ma says eat broccoli, cereal and carrots.
But God gave us tasteys for maple ice cream.
God gave us fingers—Ma says, "Use your hanky."
God gave us puddles—Ma says, "Don't splash."
Ma says, "Be quiet, your father is sleeping."
But God gave us garbage can covers to crash.
God gave us fingers—Ma says, "Put your gloves on."
God gave us raindrops—Ma says, "Don't get wet."
Ma says be careful, and don't get too near to
Those lovely strange dogs that God gave us to pet.
God gave us fingers—Ma says, "Go wash 'em."
But God gave us coal bins and nice dirty bodies.
And I ain't too smart, but there's one thing for certain—
Either Ma's wrong or else God is.[2]

I suppose all children feel this way at times. They want to play in the dirt. We say that's wrong. They want to yell and be rowdy. We say that's wrong. They want to go out and play instead of pick up their room. We say that's wrong. Every normal, curious, or interesting thing they want to do is considered wrong by some adult. But there is nothing wrong with getting dirty, yelling, and playing outside. In fact, we should enjoy seeing our children do these things. Our task is to help them do these things at appropriate times so they don't play in the mud with their best clothes on or yell during church or while they're at the neighbors' house.

Children need to be trained to be reasonably clean, neat, and mannerly—but don't overdo it. And don't jump to the conclusion that every time your children do something childish they are being bad or disobedient. Before you discipline your children for misbehaving, ask yourself if they're just being normal kids.

Normal children also act up when their physical needs aren't met. Hungry children, children who are tired, and children who have been cooped up in the backseat of the family car tend to fight more than children who are well rested, fed, and have had some good physical exercise.

WHAT ABOUT SIN?

If you are a Christian parent, you may be thinking, "But what about sin? I know there are emotional and normal reasons children misbehave, but don't they ever do anything just because they are sinful?" You bet they do! We all do things because we are sinful. But how does sin work in children? Can we just chalk up every disobedience to their sinful nature and ignore other causes of the problem? I think not.

Sin influences children in two ways. First, when we parents have trouble meeting our children's needs for love, confidence, worth, and constructive activity, we are programming them to misbehave. Our sinfulness or inability to meet our children's needs makes them more likely to misbehave in order to gain attention, power, or feelings of perfection.

The second influence is our children's own sinfulness. Even children who are deeply loved may still want to be the absolute center of attention. Even children who feel relatively confident may want to control others or always have their own way. And even children who have a good sense of worth and value may be perfectionistic and always want to win or be the very best. In other words, there is something in human nature that makes every child (and every adult, for that matter) want to be number one. We all have a sense of pride or selfishness; that is the essence of our sinful nature.

Think back to the biblical story of Adam and Eve.[3] Satan tempted them by saying, "When you eat this fruit your eyes will be opened and you will be like God." He was, in essence, saying, "You won't have to be finite and limited. You can know everything God does. You can be number one." And sure enough, Adam and Eve decided they weren't satisfied being the apex of God's created order and living under God's direction in a beautiful garden. They wanted to be number one. That's the way our children's sinfulness works.

Think of the last time you watched a group of children playing soccer. Did you overhear your child and her teammates run onto the field saying, "I hope we have a lot of fun and enjoy ourselves, but we really don't care if we win or lose"? I doubt it. They wanted to win, to feel confident and powerful. Or think how your oldest child reacted when your second child was born. Your firstborn may have been thrilled to have a new little brother or sister. But it probably wasn't long before he started picking on the little one, resenting him, or acting more baby-like himself. That's because your first child wanted to be your *most* loved or valued child. To him, his baby brother or sister seemed to be a rival for your love. Or consider such a simple thing as doing chores around the house. It is part of nearly every child's selfish nature to be bored with work and want someone else to do it.

Children rarely misbehave for just one reason. Instead, their misbehaviors are caused by a combination of their inborn temperaments, their normal childishness, and their own sinful tendencies, as well as our failure to fully meet their needs. Take, for example, a fifteen-year-old girl who becomes sexually promiscuous. The background for her promiscuity is her normal adolescent sexual development and desire to be liked by boys. She is at a stage when she is maturing sexually and should be interested in boys. But what if she has a lousy relationship with her father? What if he abandoned the family or is such a workaholic or so demanding that she doesn't feel loved by him? That will push her to find attention from the boys she dates in order to compensate for the love she isn't receiving from her father. But even though it's normal for teenagers to develop sexually, and even though her father isn't meeting her need for love, this girl's own sinfulness is also part of the picture. Not every girl whose father ignores her ends up sleeping with every guy she dates. This girl is saying, "I want attention and excitement now, even if I have to lower my standards to do it."

In similar ways, most of your children's misbehavior will be caused by a mixture of their inborn temperament, their normal struggles, your difficulty meeting their needs, and their own sin or selfishness. If you are spending a lot of time with your children, and they seem to feel pretty loved and confident and valuable but still occasionally act selfish or rebellious, there's a good chance you are seeing their innate sinfulness in action.

RECAP

This chapter finished answering the question, "Why do children misbehave?" They misbehave because:

- They are normal.
- They are born with temperaments that program them to act in certain ways.
- They have a sinful nature—a selfish bent. In a nutshell, they want to have their own way and be number one.

Most misbehaviors are triggered by a combination of the causes we have discussed in the last two chapters.

Notes

1. Debbie was what researchers Alexander Thomas and Stella Chess call an "easy child." Richard was a "slow to warm up" boy. Their book is entitled *Temperament and Development* (New York: Brunner/Mazel, 1977). In another book, *Your Child's Hidden Needs*, I discuss the most common temperament types (Revell, 1990).

2. Shel Silverstein, *Where The Sidewalk Ends* (New York: Harper Collins, 1974).

3. Genesis 3:1–7.

CHAPTER 4

Discipline or Punishment?

God is the perfect parent. The way God, our heavenly Father, loves and disciplines his earthly children can give us some great ideas for rearing our children. To demonstrate this point when I'm lecturing I often ask a group of parents, "Does God punish his children?" Almost immediately, most members of the audience nod yes. A few cautiously shake their heads in disagreement and the rest have a suspicious look that says, "You have to be careful when a psychologist asks you a question." So let me ask you the same question. "Does God, our heavenly Parent, punish his children?"

No, God doesn't punish his children. God *disciplines* his children, but there is a world of difference between discipline and punishment. God's righteousness requires that sin be punished, but Christ took that punishment once and for all when he was crucified two thousand years ago. God must punish those who don't take advantage of Christ's payment for their sins, but all punishment for the sins of his children has already been inflicted.

God never tells his children, "You sinned against me. I am angry. I am going to get even by punishing you!" Instead, he says, "You have sinned. I love you. I took out all of my righteous anger toward your sin on Christ at the cross. Since you are my child, I am going to discipline you to help you grow and mature." Read these verses carefully and you will begin to see the difference between God's punishment and his discipline.

Punishment:

I will punish the world for its evil, the wicked for their sins. I will put an end to the arrogance of the haughty and will humble the pride of the ruthless.[1]

Discipline:

> My son, do not make light of the Lord's discipline, and do not
> lose heart when he rebukes you, because the Lord disciplines
> those he loves, and he punishes [better translated *disciplines*]
> everyone he accepts as a son. Endure hardship as discipline;
> God is treating you as sons. . . . Our fathers disciplined us for a
> little while as they thought best; but God disciplines us for our
> good, that we may share in his holiness.[2]

Notice the differences between discipline and punishment.
First, the *purpose* of punishment is to inflict pain as a penalty or to balance the scales of justice. In contrast, the purpose of discipline is to
help a person mature and grow. Second, the *focus* of punishment is
largely on the past. It says, "You misbehaved back then. Now you
have to pay." Discipline focuses largely on the future. It says, "I want
you to learn from your mistake to respond differently in the future."
Although discipline may look at the past, its primary emphasis is to
redirect the disciplined one in the future. Third, the *attitude* of the
parent when punishing is anger (in God's case, righteous anger),
while discipline is done out of love. Finally, the child's *response* to punishment and discipline is different. The natural reaction to angry
punishment is fear, guilt, and resentment. The response to discipline,
even firm discipline, is love, security, and respect.

Unfortunately, most English translations of the Bible use "discipline" and "punishment" interchangeably. Consequently, some
passages, including one part of the Hebrews passage above, may read
as though God punishes his children when he actually doesn't. If you
read those verses in context and keep the distinction between "punish" and "discipline" in mind, you can interpret those passages more
accurately. Table 1 summarizes the differences between discipline
and punishment.

Just as God never punishes his children, we should never punish ours. We should discipline them, of course, and sometimes our
discipline will be firm and painful. But that is different from punishing. The Greek word for *discipline* in the New Testament can actually be translated "to train" or "to teach." Discipline is the whole
process of helping children grow up, mature, and develop. Unlike
punishment, which comes only after a misdeed, discipline includes

Table 1
PUNISHMENT AND DISCIPLINE

	Punishment	*Discipline*
Purpose	To inflict penalty for an offense (Matthew 25:46)	To train for correction and maturity (Hebrews 12:5–10)
Focus	Past misdeeds (2 Thessalonians 1:7–9)	Future correct deeds (Proverbs 3:11–12)
Parent's Attitude	Hostility and frustration (Isaiah 13:9–11)	Love and concern (Revelation 3:19)
Resulting Behavior	Outward conformity or rebellion	Growth (Titus 2:11–14)
Resulting Emotion in the Child	Fear, guilt, or hostility (Hebrews 12:18–21)	Security, love, and respect (Hebrews 12:22–24; 1 John 4:18–19)

training our children and teaching them *before* they get into trouble. Perhaps the best way to summarize the difference between discipline and punishment is to remember this: *Punishment is the work of a judge. Discipline is the work of a mother or father.* Unfortunately, most of us take on both of these roles, depending on how we feel at a given moment.

I remember the first time I disciplined our son totally out of love and for his welfare rather than punishing him in anger. Richard was an active toddler who discovered it was fun and adventurous to mountainclimb up the pantry shelves in our kitchen. Since the risk of serious harm was imminent, we decided we couldn't let Richard fall and learn his lesson the hard way. So we told him to stop climbing. Richard obediently came down, but before long he was up there again. One day I was in the living room when I heard Richard working his way up the pantry shelves. I got mad. I thought, "What's the matter with that boy? I've told him a dozen times to stay out of there!" I felt like grabbing him and giving him a good spanking. But then I caught myself.

Since I was beginning to understand the difference between God's punishment and his discipline, I had a brief inner dialogue with myself. *Narramore*, I asked, *do you want to punish your son in anger to vent your hostility and get even with him for disobeying you? Or do you want to lovingly correct him and give him an example of how God, his heavenly Father corrects him?* I quickly answered my own question by saying to myself, *Frankly, I'd like to do both. I would like to swat him a good one in anger for me and then lovingly discipline him for his own good.*

I knew that wouldn't work, of course, and I really did want to become a more loving father. I counted to twenty to cool off my anger and frustration, walked into the kitchen, and lovingly but firmly picked Richard off the fifth shelf and told him, "Richard, it's dangerous to climb up here. Mom and Dad have told you not to climb up on the shelves. I'm going to have to discipline you." Then I gave him a couple of good, medium-sized swats.

Richard immediately reacted differently than he had to previous spankings. The minute I looked in his eyes I could tell that he wasn't afraid of me. Don't get me wrong. He didn't smile and say, "Thanks, Dad. That was fun. Let's do it again." The Bible says, "No discipline seems pleasant at the time, but painful."[3] But in the past, when I had punished Richard in anger, I saw fear in his eyes. This time he was peaceful and unafraid.

Punishment may make your children change temporarily, because they are intimidated and afraid. If I had angrily spanked Richard, he probably would have stopped climbing for the moment. But even when angry punishment forces obedience, it makes children resentful, discouraged, and afraid. Let's face it: It's scary to have an adult three times your size mad at you. And it hurts to be angrily accused or attacked by a parent. Since children base so many of their feelings about themselves on our approval, it's upsetting to them to have us turn on them in anger.

Angry punishment also breaks the loving relationship that children need in order to want to obey. And it can stir up inner rebellion even when they are outwardly obedient—as one little boy whose mother angrily forced him to sit in the corner stubbornly told his mom, "Inside I'm still standing up!" Other children who are punished in anger rebel later. They silently retort, "I'll show you" or "Just wait until I'm eighteen!" It may feel good temporarily to vent our anger at our children, but their internal anxiety, depression, or delayed rebellion is too high a price to pay.

ARE YOU PUNISHING OR DISCIPLINING?

Let's say that for the last hour while you have been trying to take a nap or talk on the phone your son and daughter have been fighting about which TV channel to watch. You reach your boiling point, put your hand over the phone, and angrily yell, "I'm sick and tired of your fighting. You've been at each other all day. Now go to your rooms and stay there until I tell you to come out!"

Answer these four questions and you can tell whether you were punishing or disciplining. First, what were you feeling when you yelled at your children? Love or anger? Next, what did you focus on, their past squabbling or their future correct behavior? Third, what was your purpose? Were you trying to help them grow, or trying to get even with them and make them pay for their misdeeds? And fourth, what was their response? Did they accept your correction because you spoke firmly, but politely, or did they get angry or become afraid or depressed?

If you are like most parents, your answers reflect a mixture of discipline and punishment. Of course you wanted to help your children change. But didn't you also want them to suffer and pay for their misdeeds? Of course you wanted to train them for better future behavior. But weren't you also trying to get in their face and make them feel guilty by focusing on how bad they had been behaving all day? And of course you love your children, but at the moment you sent them to their rooms, weren't you angry and wanting to get even? And didn't your children react to your punishment with at least a little fear, guilt, or anger instead of love and respect? If so, you were punishing them instead of disciplining.

Before we go on to specific techniques of discipline in chapter 5, I want to be very clear about this point. You will get better results with firm, loving discipline than you will with angry punishment. The specific techniques of discipline you choose will not be nearly as important as your attitude and the way you apply them. That's why we have had many great parents long before we had any "experts" write books on parenting. Some parents just naturally find it easy to be both firm and loving. Most of us, however, have to work at that! It's hard to discipline when our instinct is to punish. I also want to be sure you know that when I recommend loving discipline I am not encouraging you to be soft or permissive. Loving discipline can be very firm and painful; it's just carried out in a sensitive, caring manner.

Here's a different way to handle children's fighting. Restrain your angry impulse, wait until you calm down, and then firmly tell them, "Kids, I don't want you to keep fighting. If you can't settle down and work things out, you will have to go to your rooms until you learn to get along."

When you discipline this way, your words may be similar or even identical to those you use when you punish in anger, but your attitude, focus, and purpose will be different. This time you are focusing on the future by telling them, "You will have to go to your rooms until you learn to get along." This time you are speaking firmly but lovingly instead of yelling and threatening. And this time your purpose is different. You aren't trying to get even with them because they upset you. You are training them to help them grow up and get along better.

Let's take another encounter with young children. Your toddler has just pulled all of your makeup out of the drawer and spread it over the bedroom floor. You have had a hard day, and when you discover the mess, you angrily blurt out, "Robyn, how many times have I told you to stay out of there? I'm sick and tired of your getting into my things. You have been causing problems all day. Now go to your room!" Head down and teary-eyed, Robyn heads for bed, *punished* for her actions.

Now let's say you have had a better day, and Robyn empties the contents of your makeup drawer onto the floor. In a calm but firm voice you tell her, "Robyn, Mother has told you not to take her makeup out of the drawer. I will have to discipline you so you will remember not to do that again. You will have to go to your room to remember not to do that again." Robyn was sent to her room both times, but this time you were not angry, and you *disciplined* Robyn for her actions.

Notice that you can use exactly the same corrective action (like sending Robyn to her room) for either discipline or punishment.

The key isn't the type of correction you use, it's the way you carry it out. The first time you focused on Robyn's past. You told her she had been causing problems all day. The second time you focused on the future. You told her you wanted her to do better next time. The first time you wanted Robyn to suffer for her bad behavior. The second time you corrected her so she would learn obedience for her own good. With God as our model, we should discipline our children to help them mature, but we should never punish them to frighten them, get even with them, or make them pay for their misdeeds.

God's discipline works like this:

- He sets guidelines for behavior that are not his personal whims but are for our good and are in accordance with his holy nature.
- He reaches out to us and removes all punishment for our sins on the basis of Christ's death on the cross.
- He tells his children of the negative consequences of sin, but he doesn't threaten us with punishment or rejection.
- When he needs to discipline us, he does it firmly, but in love. He disciplines to instruct us, not to vent his anger or gain revenge.

God really trains us for our own good. He never takes out his frustrations on us and he patiently guides us to maturity. Your home will be revolutionized if you begin to discipline your children with the same attitude in which God disciplines you.

"THERE IS NO FEAR IN LOVE"

Since fear is such a universal reaction to punishment (not discipline), let's take a few minutes to think about the role of fear in training children. There has been a lot of misunderstanding in the church about the role of fear. One Christian author wrote:

> If I were to ask, "Which emotion should fathers and mothers use to counter Satan's appeal?" you'd come back with the sweet reply, "LOVE." That sounds very nice and proper, doesn't it? Well, I'm sorry—that's NOT the emotion. We need something more forceful than parental love. There's only one emotion that is greater—FEAR. . . . Fear is the one great emotion to which

everyone responds. Fear alone can check the awesome forces unleashed in teens.[4]

This author goes on to recommend slapping a teenage daughter, using a switch on the bare legs of children, and hitting a teenage boy "flush on the jaw" when he talks back to his mother. I understand this author's concern with getting children to obey, but his approach is absolutely incorrect, unbiblical, and cruel. It is a harmful misunderstanding of how God relates to us and how we should rear children. According to the Bible, God's children should have a reverential trust in him and a respect for his authority, but we should never be afraid of him. The apostle John wrote: "There is no fear in love. But perfect love drives out fear, because fear has to do with punishment."[5] And Paul told young Timothy, "For God did not give us a spirit of timidity (fear); but a spirit of power of love and of self-discipline."[6]

Few things could be clearer. John doesn't say fear is greater than love; he says just the opposite. Love drives out fear. Then, John connects fear to punishment. Since Christ has taken our punishment, we have absolutely no reason to be afraid of God. God lovingly asks for our obedience. He tells us about the consequence of sin and the advantages of Christian living. And he disciplines us. But he doesn't lose his temper and stomp around heaven, threatening to drop a star on our head. And he expects us not to act that way with our children as well.

Fear actually drives people away. Many Christians have lost out on a vital relationship with God because they were afraid of him. Have you ever sinned and then had that vague, fearful thought, *Sometime, somehow, God is going to get even with me*? This is natural, since most of us were brought up on a "balanced scale" system. Each time we misbehaved, the scale tipped to the "bad behavior" side. Once we were punished, the scale evened up and again read, "Accounts even. Paid in full." But for all those who trust in Christ, God has balanced the scale forever.

Some people are confused about this because the Bible sometimes seems to condone fear. But whenever the Bible uses fear in reference to God's children it is used in a positive way to mean "respect" or "reverential trust." When Proverbs says, "The fear of the Lord is the beginning of wisdom,"[7] and "The fear of the Lord leads to life,"[8] for example, it doesn't mean that we should feel panicky and anxious around God. It means that respect or reverential trust in God and an awareness of his holiness make us wise and help us live closer to him. The Bible also says that those who are not God's children *should* be afraid. But it never shows God motivating his children with anxious, upsetting fear.

TEACHING RESPECT WITHOUT CREATING FEAR

After I talked about the difference between punishment and discipline at a meeting of parents, a father stood up and said, "It's fine to talk about this love stuff, but you can't lollygag around when children are challenging your authority. You have to teach them to respect you and show them who's the boss. I think fear and anger is the only way to do that."

I agree that we need to teach children to respect us. And I agree that there are times to firmly exercise our authority. But fear and anger aren't the ways to teach those lessons. Take, for example, teaching your children to respect your advice about looking both ways for traffic when crossing the street. You can anxiously yell, "Look out! Here comes a car!" every time they near the street and I'm sure that will teach your children to be careful. But it will also

make them fearful. They won't be able to go near a street corner without their palms sweating or their heart racing. On the other hand, you can calmly tell them, "We look both ways before we cross the street so we won't get hit by a car." By looking both ways and calmly telling them to do the same, you teach your children to be alert to danger without turning them into nervous wrecks. That's the

45

way God works with us. He tells us that sin has hurtful consequences, but he doesn't anxiously shout in our ear each time we are about to do something wrong. And he doesn't scare his children with threats of punishment.

The same principle applies if your junior higher or high schooler sasses you. Since you want him to respect you and your authority, you clearly need to do something. You have two options: You can threaten him, or you can sit down and have a sane conversation in which you both try to understand him and let him know that his behavior is unacceptable.

This is one place I differ with my friend, Dr. James Dobson, author of the best-seller, *Dare to Discipline*. In a section on teaching children to respect their parents, Jim tells a hilarious story of how his mother handled sassing. He says:

> The day I learned the importance of staying out of reach shines like a neon light in my mind. I made the costly mistake of "sassing" her when I was about four feet away. She wheeled around to grab something with which to hit me, and her hand landed on a girdle. She drew back and swung that abominable garment in my direction, and I can still hear it whistling through the air. The intended blow caught me across the chest, followed by a multitude of straps and buckles, wrapping themselves around my midsection. She gave me an entire thrashing with one massive blow. From that day forward, I cautiously retreated a few steps before popping off.[9]

That's a great story. And it gets a point across about parents being in charge. But notice that Jim didn't learn respect from that punishment. He still "popped off." He just retreated a few steps first. Angry punishment has that effect. It either results in fear-based conformity or teaches children to move to a safe distance before they disobey.

A better way to handle sassing is to begin by hearing your child out. Let her tell you how mad she is and why. Be strong enough to listen and take her feelings seriously without retaliating. After you have listened to her complaints tell her, "I'm sorry you're upset" or "I'm sorry I upset you." If you did something inappropriate, apologize. If you can do anything to help her feel better, do it. Once you have taken time to understand and be helpful, then tell her, "Honey, we all get upset sometimes, and that's okay. I want you to tell me when you're upset with me. But I want you to try to tell me in a different way. If you could tell me, 'Mom, I'm furious' or 'Mom, I'm mad,' instead of 'I hate you' or 'You're so stupid,' it would be easier for me to listen. When you say you hate me, I want to fight back instead of listening and trying to understand."

If you are too angry to be that patient, simply tell her, "You may not sass your mother. Go to your room until we both settle down and are able to talk this over reasonably." Then, when you do talk, listen to her hurt and calmly tell her you want her to let you know how she feels, but in a less attacking way.

If your daughter needs more firm correction, tell her, "To help you remember not to talk that way, if you do it again, I will ground you for the weekend." By respecting her right to her thoughts and feelings, but showing her how she can express them in a less destructive way, you gain her respect as you discipline. Remember, your goal isn't to frighten her or drive a wedge between you. It is to help her be more polite next time.

I don't mean that you should allow children to recklessly or violently express their anger. There are times when each of us, including children, must restrain our feelings. But in an intimate parent-child relation, your children should feel accepted and loved enough to be honest about their feelings—even their negative ones.

There is one more way you can increase the likelihood that you will discipline your children respectfully rather than in anger: Sit down while you discipline. Do you nearly always stand up when you correct your children? If you do, it's probably because you want to use your superior size to frighten them into obedience. If you really want to discipline in love, try sitting down on the same level as your children rather than towering over them like a giant. In fact, it's always good to be on eye-level when you are talking with your children.

WHAT ABOUT *MY* FEELINGS?

Disciplining in love and hearing what our children have to say before we react sounds great, but if you are like me, sometimes you don't feel like disciplining in love or listening calmly. Sometimes you just get angry. For now, I simply want to make three points. First, we will all occasionally get angry and feel like punishing our children to get even instead of disciplining them for their own good. That's normal. Second, as Christians, we should aspire to become more loving parents. Third, there *are* ways of learning to control our anger so that we can follow God's model of disciplining in love. In chapter 10, we will look at what you can do when you get angry with your children and what you can do when you don't feel like disciplining in love.

RECAP

Our discipline should be modeled after God's discipline of his children.

- God disciplines his children, but he never punishes them.
- The purpose of punishment is justice and revenge.
- The purpose of discipline is to train for maturity and for the child's best interest.
- Punishment is motivated by feelings of anger, whereas discipline is carried out in love.
- We should discipline our children, but we shouldn't punish them.
- Punishment creates fear, guilt, and anger in our children.
- Fear, guilt, and anger are poor motivators and create untold emotional problems. God doesn't motivate his children this way, and neither should we.
- It's important for children to respect others and to be aware of the negative consequences of their actions, but respect is entirely different from fear.

Now that we have seen the differences between discipline and punishment, it's time to learn some specific techniques that you can apply to the daily hassles you face at home. That's the topic of the next few chapters.

Notes

1. Isaiah 13:11.
2. Hebrews 12:5–7, 10.

3. Hebrews 12:11.

4. C. S. Lovett, *What's a Parent to Do?* (Baldwin Park: Personal Christianity Chapel, 1971), 61.

5. 1 John 4:18.

6. 2 Timothy 1:7.

7. Proverbs 9:10.

8. Proverbs 19:23.

9. James Dobson, *Dare to Discipline* (Wheaton: Tyndale House, 1970), 16.

CHAPTER 5

Three Tools for Toddler Taming and Child Training

Some psychologists, believe it or not, spend most of their lives training white rats to obey. These furry little creatures make great research subjects, since experimental psychologists can do things with rats that they can't do with humans. In one experiment, researchers place a rat in a maze and put two goal boxes at the other end. If the rat traipses down the laboratory runway and pushes the target box on the right-hand side, a pellet of food drops down and he is rewarded for his efforts. If he pushes the target on the left, nothing happens. Being relatively intelligent, after a few trips down the runway our little white friend learns to always push the target on the right. The researcher trained him by rewarding the behavior he wanted and not rewarding the behavior he didn't want.

Children learn a little like rats. They can be trained to pick up after themselves, make their beds, stop fighting, stop throwing tantrums, arrive at meals on time, and do their chores if we just implement the following simple but powerful training tools: (1) not rewarding misbehavior, (2) rewarding good behavior, and (3) modeling desirable behavior. Psychologists call these tools *extinction*, *rewards*, and *imitation*.

REMOVE REWARDS FOR MISBEHAVIOR

A *reward* is any little goodie a child likes—a piece of candy, attention, money, a compliment, getting his own way, or making his little brother cry after he teases him. Let's say you just told your daughter that she can't have a Twinkie before dinner. Pleading in a mournful voice, she says, "But Mom, I'm starving. I haven't had anything to eat *all day*." When you kindly tell her, "I'm sorry honey, but you know our rule—no snacks before supper," she keeps whining and complaining. Every time you tell her no she intensifies her efforts. Since you've had a hard day and your nerves are on the edge, you finally cave in and tell her in a resigned voice, "Okay, but just this once!"

What have you taught your daughter? As sure as a psychologist trains his white rat to hit the goal box at the right side of the runway, you have taught her that if she wants a Twinkie before dinner, all she has to do is whine until you can't take it anymore. In fact, you may as well put a note on the refrigerator door that reads:

Dear Jan,

If you would like a snack between meals, please fuss, whine, and cry until I am on the verge of a nervous breakdown. Then you may have one.

Love, Mom

If you want your children to stop an annoying behavior, the first thing you must do is to stop rewarding them for it. When a behavior stops because it hasn't been rewarded, we say that that behavior has been *extinguished*. Extinction is a wonderful tool for your child training kit. It's as basic to discipline as a pair of pliers or a screwdriver is to fixing things around the house. Extinction won't solve all problems by itself, but when you use it along with a couple of other training techniques we'll discuss later, it is a very powerful tool. Once you know how to use it, extinction can help you:

- stop temper tantrums
- eliminate unnecessary crying, whining, and complaining
- teach children to pick up after themselves
- reduce sibling fights
- overcome procrastination

Stop and think about it. How many of your children's undesirable actions are you unknowingly rewarding? What do you do when you find the milk, half a loaf of stale bread, and an opened jar of peanut butter on the kitchen table? If you are like most parents, you immediately replace the lid on the peanut butter, put the milk back in the refrigerator where it belongs, and wipe up the crumbs. When your children come home you may jump on them for leaving a mess, but by then it's too late. You have already rewarded their irresponsibility by picking up after them. You are training them to misbehave.

Here's a better way. Simply leave the food on the table until your children get home, then tell them to put it back where it belongs. I realize the milk may go sour and the bread might get crusty, but that's not your problem. The next morning simply tell your children, "I'm sorry, but the milk went sour when you left it out yesterday so we don't have any for breakfast." Or, if you don't want the rest of your family to go without milk, simply tell the offender, "Since you left the milk out and it went bad, you will have to pay me for the replacement I bought." Both of these tactics avoid rewarding your children for their messiness.

If your child keeps "forgetting" to do her chores or take care of her things, you have probably been rewarding her. Don't you pick up after her, remind her to get her things, or bring her forgotten papers to school when she frantically calls from the pincipal's office? Why should she put much effort into remembering when she knows you will do it for her?

Or take another common problem with pre-school children—temper tantrums. Children throw tantrums for one of three reasons. First, to gain attention. It's hard to ignore a child who is screaming at the top of his lungs and banging his head against the kitchen wall. Second, children throw tantrums to get their own way, or to gain power and control over us. Finally, children throw tantrums to gain revenge on us. When we don't give in to their wishes, they think, "I may not get my way, but at least I'll make my parents miserable for not giving me what I want."

Let's say you have just told your son he can't go outside to play. Screaming at the top of his lungs, he throws himself on the floor and flails hysterically. I can assure you, he *isn't* looking for attention! He is looking for power and control. He wants you to change your mind and do things his way. If you give in and let him go outside you may gain some momentary quiet, but you will have also rewarded him for his tantrum and increased the chances he will throw another tantrum the next time he wants his way. If you consistently refuse to reward your son's tantrums, he will conclude they don't work, and he'll be less likely to throw another one.

Some parents think spanking is a good way to stop a tantrum. But what if your child is throwing the tantrum to gain your attention? Although there are times for spanking, this isn't one of them. The moment you spank him, you reward him with attention. Even though spankings are painful, some children are willing to endure the pain to receive the reward of our attention. While a spanking may temporarily stop disruptive behavior, the next time the child feels a need for attention, he'll misbehave again. A better tactic is to ignore the tantrum. Go on with your work as though nothing is happening. Actors don't put on a play when no paying customers show up, and your children won't put on a tantrum show when nobody is paying attention.

Let me warn you about one thing, however. Don't be surprised if, the first few times you ignore your children's tantrums, they yell louder. Since yelling has worked their entire lives, they may conclude that your hearing has gone bad, and that once they yell loud enough you will give in! But don't do it. If it's too upsetting to be near them, go to another room. One mother told me that when she went to another room her tantrum-throwing two-year-old promptly followed, laid down at her feet, and resumed crying. When she changed rooms, he followed her again. She finally went into the bathroom and locked the door. When he *still* didn't stop, she took a nice long shower so she couldn't hear him over the running water. When she came out, he was fine!

After another mother learned this technique, she continued her housework and started singing quietly the next time her son threw a tantrum. After a few seconds he stopped in the middle of his act, looked directly at his mother and yelled, "Stop it! Can't you see I'm trying to be angry?" He couldn't believe his mom wasn't falling for his ploy.

You may not want to take a shower or start singing every time your children have a tantrum, but you get my point. Whatever you do, don't try to force children to stop a tantrum. The minute you do, you give them the very attention or control they want. This, of course, may not be possible when you are in a public place. You can't ignore a child who is rolling cans of food or eggs down the aisles at your local supermarket! We will see how to handle that sort of situation in chapter 6. But for situations at home, the best thing to do is not reward the tantrum.

When you get to the end of this chapter, why not make a list of some things your children do that you would like to change? Then think of how you may unknowingly be rewarding those behaviors by giving them exactly what they want.

A Word of Caution

Now that you know that rewards and extinction can be powerful tools for training children, please realize that they can also be seriously abused. In southern California, a parenting movement has sprung up that asserts a supposedly biblical approach to parenting. Although the course has many fine points and scriptural qualities, it also has some potentially disastrous flaws.

The authors of this parenting movement claim that since children are born sinful, parents must teach them from the very beginning of life that they are not going to be the center of the world. Parents are told that they should often ignore their babies' cries for milk or attention, and only feed them on a schedule set up by the parents. When you first think about it, that seems to make sense. Babies are demanding. But the authors push this point to an extreme and combine it with the principle of extinction. They end up saying that all children should be put on a rigid feeding schedule of approximately every three to three and a half hours, starting from the time they are one week of age. The rationale is that if you allow babies to eat when they wish, you are letting them control you instead of teaching them to give up their selfish ways. By feeding them on a schedule, the mother can extinguish this selfishness.

But, wait a minute. Who said that babies should be fed only on a feeding schedule? The Bible certainly doesn't. Babies have tiny stomachs and digestive systems, and when they are hungry, they need nourishment. Besides that, mothers who do not nurse more frequently may actually begin to produce less milk, leading to undernourishment for the baby. In fact, some infants on this rigid schedule have been hospitalized with as much as two pounds of weight loss during the first few weeks of life.

Another feature of this parenting program is the recommendation that babies should often be ignored when they cry. Again, the motive is to force the baby to realize he is not the center of the world. The authors claim that to pick up the baby when he is crying may reinforce his efforts to control or manipulate the parents. Consequently, they believe that leaving the baby alone when he cries will extinguish that sinful behavior.

From a simple behavioral perspective, this makes sense. If you don't want your baby to cry, never reward him for crying and he should stop. But again, we need to think twice. We aren't rearing white rats. We are rearing precious children. Babies cry because they have needs and hurts and pains. Crying is their only way of communicating. An infant can't say, "I have gas pains. Will you burp me?" or "I'm hungry. Will you feed me?" or "I'm frightened and alone. Will you hold me?" Crying is his way to send a message. If we ignore a crying baby we are telling him, "I don't care if you are frightened or hurting. I have my own life to live, and I am not going to interrupt it to help you." We are extinguishing our baby's hope that the world is a good place, that he can be heard and understood by another human being, that when he is in need, someone will care and help.

This is why it is so important to understand our children's needs for love, confidence, and worth. If we overlook these needs, we will try to shape just their behavior and be in danger of rearing well-behaved, empty, sad, isolated souls. In fact, some major research studies show that parenting styles like these produce an opposite and undesired effect. For example, one study shows that crying infants who are picked up and provided with close bodily contact actually cry less as toddlers and are able to communicate their needs better than toddlers who were not picked up when they cried as babies. Learning as infants that their communication efforts (crying) brought results gave them confidence as they grew older that their words would also be heard. Babies whose cries weren't responded to either gave up, lost hope, became quiet out of despair, or cried and threw more tantrums because they still wanted their parents to respond.[1]

In the same way, infants who are fed according to their own signals of hunger have fewer feeding problems and adjust better to the family schedule as toddlers.[2] Based on past experience, they do not become anxious and upset, because they know that Mother will be there to feed them.

Research indicates that failing to respond to a baby's cues can do significant emotional damage to her. So, before you decide to extinguish an undesirable behavior, determine whether it reflects a God-given need such as food or love. If it does, attend to that need first. After that, you can work to change the behavior. Some behaviors, such as crying, that shouldn't be ignored during a baby's infancy, *can* be ignored a year or so later. I'll say more about that in chapter 14.

REWARD GOOD BEHAVIOR

The next step, after attending to your child's unmet needs and removing rewards for misbehavior, is to start rewarding positive behaviors. Let's say that one Saturday morning your usually messy twelve-year-old cleans up his room and puts all of his clothes away. After that, he picks up his baseball cards from the family room and washes the dirty cereal bowl he left in the kitchen the night before. If you don't pass out from shock, and if you ever want him to repeat these actions, you better find some way to reward him for his helpfulness—quick! Tell him, "Thanks for straightening the family room, Todd. I sure appreciate your help." Along with your thanks, give him a hug—as long as his friends aren't around! You might also tell him, "Since you helped me so much, let's go downtown later and see if we can find that new pair of soccer shoes you've been talking about."

You rewarded your son in several ways. Your thanks and hug are *social rewards*. A social reward is any human action like hugging, praising, listening, or spending time together. The new shoes are a *nonsocial reward*. A nonsocial reward is an object like candy, money, or toys. By using both social and nonsocial rewards, you've made Todd feel much more willing to help you clean the house again. Of course, there are the natural rewards of living in a clean house and helping your parents. But for most children, that is not enough!

A psychologist friend of mine teaches parents this positive principle by urging them to "Catch your children being good!" He means that instead of rewarding children for undesirable actions, we should catch them in a good act and reward them for it. I'm not saying you should run out and buy your children a chocolate sundae every time they behave correctly. That's impossible. Besides that, children shouldn't think they deserve a reward for everything they do. But when children (or adults, for that matter) are learning a new task or taking on a new responsibility, they need lots of rewards to motivate them. Once desirable behaviors become a habit, rewards are not needed as often. The combination of your child's own inner satisfaction and an occasional reward from someone else is enough to keep the new behaviors going.

To make sure rewards work, you will need to do three things. First, reward your children immediately after they perform the desired behavior. If you want to be sure your son removes his clothes and baseball cards from the family room a second time, it won't work to wait a few weeks and then tell him, "Oh, by the way, Todd, I appreciate your picking up after yourself last month." By then it's too late; he won't associate the reward with his next behavior. Think of your own experience. Wives, if your husband compliments you on a new hairstyle the first time he sees you, his reinforcement makes you want to keep looking nice. But if he waits until your hair is frazzled and says, "Honey, your hair sure looked nice last month," you probably won't be overjoyed! Husbands, if your wife brings you a cold lemonade and tells you, "The yard looks terrific," while the grass clippings are still covering your shoes, you are encouraged to keep chasing the mower. But if she waits two months to thank you, chances are great that the yard will look like a jungle before you mow it again.

The second key is to reinforce small improvements. Don't wait until your toddler can dress himself completely before you reward him for his efforts. Start by telling him, "Good for you!" for merely bringing you his clothes. After he has done that, you might smile broadly while he is putting on his pants by himself. Once he's learned to put on his pants, withhold any more reinforcement until he learns to tie his shoes. Eventually, reward him for dressing himself completely. By breaking a complex job into small, manageable parts, and rewarding each part separately, you help your children learn at a pace they can handle.

The third key to making rewards work is to stop reinforcing undesirable behaviors while you reward desirable ones. You won't teach your son to pick up after himself by rewarding him one day and picking up after him the next. But if you take away the reward of *your* picking up at the same time you reward *his* picking up, you will be well on your way to changing his messiness.

In chapter 9, we will discuss more about rewards—especially the pros and cons of using money or other nonsocial objects as rewards. For now, I simply want to show how rewards can be one step in training your children to do what you want them to do.

WHO IS TRAINING WHOM?

Although I've never known a rat to train a psychologist, if you aren't careful, your children will use rewards and extinction to train you. Consider, for example, getting your children to the dinner table. If you call softly, "Jayden, it's time for dinner," chances are that Jayden won't pay much attention. So a couple of minutes later you call a little louder, "Jayden, it's time for dinner!" When Jayden still doesn't respond, you shout, "Jayden! Get in here this minute if you're going to eat." Finally, Jayden drags himself to the table.

Notice what is happening. When Jayden doesn't come on your first call, he is extinguishing your polite behavior. But your yelling is rewarded when he appears. Jayden has trained you to yell.

Now, let me ask a question. Who ought to be training whom? Instead of Jayden training you to yell louder, why not train Jayden to come the first time he is called in a polite tone of voice?

Nagging is another example of children training us. On Friday evening Mother says, "Remember, Dave, you're taking out the trash

tomorrow." The next morning she reminds him again, "Don't forget the trash." Later in the day she asks anxiously, "Have you taken care of the trash yet?" Finally, Dave gives a disgusted "Okay!" and empties the trash. Mother thinks, "That boy. You have to remind him a dozen times or he won't do anything." While she may think her nagging is training Dave, actually, Dave has taught his mother that she must nag him several times before he will obey.

How much better it would be if Dave could be taught to carry out the trash the first time, or better yet, without even being reminded. I will show you how to do that, as well as how to get your children to dinner the first time you call, in chapter 7. For now, I want you to see that you may be letting your children train you into poor parenting habits instead of *your* teaching *them* good behavior. If you frequently remind your children, do their chores, or pick up after them, it is probably because they have been extinguishing your better efforts to motivate them, and rewarding you for nagging them or doing their work for them.

LIKE FATHER, LIKE SON: IMITATION IS A TRAINING TOOL

What do the following scenarios have in common: a child playing pat-a-cake, a mimicking monkey at a zoo, and a teenager who bashes mailboxes after he sees it done in a movie? They are all engaging in a form of learning through imitation, called *modeling*. The phrase, "Like father like son" captures the potential and the danger of this powerful training tool.

Children learn virtually everything by observing their moms and dads. You can tell your children to be polite at the dinner table, but if your own manners are less than exemplary, forget it. One mother entered her kitchen and discovered her son had unloaded all the food from the freezer. When his mom asked why he did that, the little boy replied, "I was defrogging the 'frigerator." He was trying to be helpful by modeling his behavior after his mom. If you want your children to refrain from certain behaviors (profanity, smoking, alcohol, gossip, etc.), but you participate in the same activities, you are a walking billboard endorsing those behaviors, regardless of what you say to your children.

Children even develop their masculine and feminine identities through imitating us. You can't teach a girl how to become a woman by telling her. She picks it up from her mother. Neither can you teach a boy how to be a man. But as he identifies with his father and imitates his behavior, he gradually takes on his attitudes and actions. Masculine and feminine roles are reinforced by good relations with the parent of the opposite sex, but children first learn their roles by observing their same-sexed parent.

© 1991 Bil Keane
Dist. by Cowles Synd., Inc.

"Why *can't* I talk like that?
Bart Simpson does!"

Modeling is both the easiest and most difficult part of training children. It's easy because we don't even have to think about it to do it. All we have to do is be ourselves, and our children pick up our attitudes and habits. It's difficult because changing our own poor habits is essential. In addition to rewarding your children's positive behavior and extinguishing their negative behavior, you need to be growing into a sensitive and mature parent so that you will be a good model for your children's behavior.

RECAP

In this chapter we have discussed three tools for changing children's behavior—*extinction*, *reward*, and *imitation*. These tools aren't new. I'm sure you have used them all already. In this chapter I have simply made these tools explicit. Let's review, to show how they work with one more common problem—children who need to learn some table manners.

1. Attitudes and actions that are rewarded or reinforced are more likely to be repeated in the future.
2. Behaviors that are not rewarded tend to weaken and become extinguished.
3. A reinforcement is anything that satisfies a goal or leads to pleasure.
   a. A social reinforcer is any type of positive interaction with another person.
   b. A nonsocial reinforcer is any material object or experience that the child enjoys.
4. To be most effective, a behavior should be reinforced soon after it occurs.
5. When teaching new behaviors, break a large task into several smaller steps and give rewards after each one.
6. When your children are learning a new behavior, reward them every time they perform the task.
7. After a desirable behavior is learned, it needs to be reinforced only occasionally.
8. Parents often unknowingly reinforce undesirable actions even though we don't approve of the behavior.
9. Children often reinforce our undesirable parental behaviors such as nagging, reminding, and picking up for our children.
10. Children learn by imitating us.

If your family is typical, the two most difficult times of the day are mealtimes and getting children out of bed and off to school in the morning. Let's apply these ten principles to a common mealtime problem.

One evening at the supper table Troy said, "Dad, gimme some more bread!" Mr. Andrews handed Troy the bread and reminded him, "You should say, 'Please pass the bread.'" Unknowingly, he was reinforcing Troy's poor manners (1 & 8). Mr. Andrews shouldn't have passed the bread when Troy said "gimme." If he had ignored the request, or calmly reminded his son, "We don't pass things unless you ask politely," Mr. Andrews wouldn't have rewarded Troy's impoliteness, and the chances of his saying "gimme" at another meal would have lessened (2). Later, Troy said, "Mom, please pass the milk." Mrs. Andrews passed the milk and complimented him for being polite. In this way, she reinforced the desired behavior (1) with both a social reward (compliment, 3a) and a nonsocial reinforcer (milk, 3b). By passing food immediately after each polite request, the Andrews are encouraging Troy's polite behavior by immediately reinforcing him (4) and by rewarding him each time he shows polite behavior (6). After Troy acquires the habit of saying "please," it won't be necessary to reward him with praise each time he is polite (7). An occasional social reward along with the regular reward of passing the food will maintain the good habit.

Notes

1. S. M. V. Bell and M. D. S. Ainsworth, "Infant crying maternal responsiveness," *Child Development* 43, (1973): 1171–90.

2. M. D. S. Ainsworth and S. M. V. Bell. "Some contemporary patterns of mother-infant interaction in the feeding situation." In J. A. Ambrose (ed.), *Stimulation in early infancy* (London: Academic, 1969), 133–170.

CHAPTER 6

Let Nature Discipline Your Child

When our daughter, Debbie, was about fifteen months of age, she started nibbling on our bathroom soap. The first time we saw her, we smiled, told her "No-no," and took the soap away. The second time we told her "No" and spanked her hand. A day or so later on a Sunday morning we found her smiling mischievously with a tooth-marked bar of soap in hand.

I was tempted to spank Debbie again so she wouldn't eat the soap and get sick. But then I realized I was about to get sucked into an unnecessary struggle. Why did I need to force Debbie to stop eating soap? After all, a little soap wasn't going to make her dangerously ill, and she seemed stubbornly bent on eating it. Besides that, if soap wasn't good for her, she would soon find out! So I restrained my impulse to correct Debbie by force, went back to the kitchen, and ate my breakfast. Debbie stayed in the bathroom to eat hers.

Twenty minutes later I heard a whimper from the bathroom. When I went to investigate, there was Debbie with her bar of soap, about one-third of it missing. When Debbie saw me, she started crying loudly. I picked her up and put her face under the bathtub faucet to wash out the soap. Bubbles kept floating out of her mouth and Debbie had a terrible look on her face. Then her lips began to swell. I felt horrible. What an awful way to neglect such a sweet, "innocent" child! Of course, I hadn't neglected Debbie at all. And as sweet as she was, Debbie really wasn't "innocent." We had forewarned her and had even given her a pat on the hand. In spite of that, she chose to disobey us.

When Debbie's lips kept swelling, Kathy phoned our family physician. He told us to apply a little Vaseline and assured us that Debbie would be fine in a few hours. We put on the Vaseline, got Debbie dressed, and headed off to church with a listless, queasy daughter. After church, the nursery worker told us, "Debbie didn't seem to be feeling very well this morning." I thought to myself, *If you only knew why!* Back at home, Debbie wouldn't eat any lunch or take a nap, although she was tired and fussy. Finally, by evening she started to recover.

That was a rough day, but later that week our disciplinary efforts were rewarded. Kathy saw Debbie pick up a bar of soap, lift it to her mouth, smell it, lick it, and then lay it down without taking a bite. To our knowledge, Debbie hasn't eaten soap since.

THE SCHOOL OF HARD KNOCKS

We've discussed three tools for training children—extinction, rewards, and imitation. Debbie's soap escapade demonstrates a fourth way: *natural consequences*. Many of your children's misbehaviors have painful built-in consequences that teach them great lessons if you stay out of the way long enough to let them learn.

If your young son is threatening to touch a hot iron, for example, don't anxiously hover over him and repeatedly warn him. Tell him once, "Don't touch that. It will hurt you." If he persists, let him touch it. He will learn two great lessons. First, that irons are hot. More importantly, that it is smart to listen to his parents!

The same tactic applies to children who don't dress warmly in cold weather, teenagers who stay out in the sun too long at the beach, and children who stuff themselves with too much food. All you need to do is warn them once of the painful natural consequences they may bring upon themselves. Then let nature run its course.

Of course, some situations are too dangerous for natural consequences. If your toddler is about to drink Liquid Plumber or fall into a swimming pool, you can't sit calmly by. If your toddler is in a situation of severe potential danger, just remove him to a safe place. Then divert his attention, remove the dangerous object, or shut the door to keep him away from danger. *Don't use natural consequences if they would result in severe or lasting injury.* Neither should we use natural consequences for things like not brushing teeth, when the resulting natural consequence— yellow, cavity-ridden teeth—may not show up for many years.

Be careful, however, in deciding what is severe or lasting injury. Those of us who are the most concerned about our children are often the most likely to overprotect them. Since we can't stand to see our daughter sick from eating soap, or worse yet, with a burn on her hand or a sunburn on her body, we try to force her to do what we know is best. But the moment we force her, we rob her of a chance to learn for herself. When she reaches adulthood she won't have us around to remind her to put on warm clothes, wear enough suntan lotion, or avoid hot objects. The sooner she learns to take care of herself the better.

The idea of natural consequences was popularized in our generation by a psychiatrist named Rudolf Dreikurs.[1] It was in the Bible, however, long before that. The prophet Jeremiah wrote, "Your wickedness will punish you."[2] The apostle Paul wrote, "A man reaps what he sows."[3] And remember the parable of the prodigal son? It illustrates natural consequences. A young man asked his father for his inheritance so he could get away from the farm and enjoy a playboy's life in another country. I'm sure that the father was aware of the pitfalls and gave his son some dire warnings. He could also have forced the boy to stay home by not giving him his inheritance. But he realized his son wouldn't grow up unless he learned some lessons the hard way, so he gave him his inheritance and let him enroll in the school of hard knocks. Sure enough, the boy ignored his father's warnings, spent his inheritance on loose living, and ended up in poverty. Things were so bad he was tempted to eat the food he had been hired to feed to pigs.[4]

When the boy returned home in poverty and broken health, his father didn't rub it in by telling him "I told you so" or lecturing the boy. That painful experience had already taught the young man more than a lecture ever would. Instead, the father threw a party.

Natural consequences are especially good for teaching children lessons about overspending their allowance, abusing their own property, and taking care of their bodies. Any time your children's actions could cause damage or loss of their own property or an immediate, nonsevere, painful impact on their lives, you usually don't need to look for other methods of correction. That's because these actions bring on their own form of pain and discipline.

Natural consequences have three great advantages over many other discipline techniques:

- They eliminate parent-child power struggles and the need to constantly warn or remind your children.
- They teach children to be responsible.
- They teach children to respect their parents.

Let's see how this works.

AVOIDING POWER STRUGGLES: IT TAKES TWO TO TANGLE

If you are like most parents, you periodically get sucked into a power struggle or a clash of wills. You tell your children what to do. They disobey, forget, or fail to follow through. You remind them several times or try to compel them, but they still don't comply. This continues until you lose your temper and force them to obey, or give up and let them have their way. In the end, nobody really wins.

A power struggle can begin with something as simple as reminding your son to wear warm clothes on a cold day. He replies, "It's not cold out. I won't need it today." "Yes you will," you tell him. "You might get sick." "No I won't," he whines in return. And the battle is on.

Power struggles are one of a parent's biggest headaches. They can happen over almost anything, but prime candidates are chores, eating, dressing, and getting off to school on time. Few things are more irritating than children who won't do something the first time we tell them. In fact, most arguments between parents and children boil down to power struggles.

If this is happening in your home, watch out. It is an escalating cycle that can go on for twenty years. In fact, when your children hit adolescence, they will just have more excuses to disregard you—and they will be better at arguing!

Children like power struggles because, if they resist long enough, they can get out of a lot of things they don't like to do. What better way is there for a teenager to avoid his chores than to keep "forgetting," or to ignore you or argue with you? Power struggles also give children a temporary sense of strength or control. What better way is there for a two-year-old to feel powerful than to say no to a six-foot giant?

There are two ways to solve power struggles. The first is to out-yell, out-threaten, and out-pressure your children. Since you are bigger, you can probably force your children to obey. But that takes an incredible amount of work and creates more problems than it solves. Even if you "win" by coercing your children, you lose because you had to fight so hard to win. Besides that, pressuring and reminding robs your children of a chance to learn some important lessons, and stirs up a lot of resentment toward you, too. Many children get even with pressuring parents by letting their grades drop or by picking friends their parents don't approve of.

A second way to solve these struggles is to avoid them! The minute your children start to suck you into a power struggle, remove yourself from the battle. Why should you have to stand by the door reminding your children to put on their coats every time they leave the house? The natural consequence of not dressing warmly is being cold and uncomfortable. All you need to do is tell your children once (not once every day, just once!) that it's important to dress warmly, then keep quiet and let them learn the hard way.

You won't believe how many hassles can be eliminated this way. I realize you are afraid your children will get sick, and you will have medical bills to pay. But wouldn't you be willing to pay one or two medical bills if it meant never having to remind them to dress warmly again? I know you may feel guilty if your son catches a cold, but you can deal with that later. For now, just remember that the big advantage natural consequences have over most other forms of discipline is that *they* do the teaching, eliminating the need for you to remind, pressure, or nag your children.

Last year I saw a great example of how this works. I was speaking at a week-long family conference at a mountain retreat just outside of Los Angeles. The mother of a preschool boy named Jeffrey was having a terrible time getting him ready for each day's activities. First, Jeffrey didn't want to get out of bed. Then he didn't want to get into the bathtub. Then he didn't want to get out. Then he wouldn't get dressed. Just as his mom reached her breaking point, she remembered what I had shared about natural consequences the day before.

She told Jeffrey, "If you don't want to get dressed you don't have to. You can go outside naked."

Jeffrey was shocked to think that his mother would let him run around a Christian conference center in the buff! But as soon as he

© 1991 Bil Keane
Dist. by Cowles Synd., Inc.

"I caught him, but not before he shocked a few neighbors."

realized she meant business, he protested, "But Mom, it's cold outside." (Notice that it is now *Jeffrey* telling his mother it's cold rather than his mother reminding Jeffrey!)

"I know it's cold, Jeffrey," his mom replied.

"But Mom, you wouldn't make me do that. You would make me get sick," Jeffrey countered. (Notice that it is now *Jeffrey* that is concerned about getting sick, not his mother!)

"No Jeffrey, *I* wouldn't be making you get sick," his mother responded. "You would be making *yourself* sick."

A serious look came over Jeffrey's face, and he immediately started dressing.

Notice how this worked. Jeffrey was trying to drag his mother into a power struggle. He was going to make her force him every step of the way. Like many children, Jeffrey took his mother's instructions as an opportunity to exercise a little control over both his own life and his mother. And his mother was about to fall into his baited trap, because she held the false assumption that it was her job to see that Jeffrey was dressed each morning.

Jeffrey and his mom were headed for years of power struggles until she decided the cold mountain air would be a better teacher than she was. When Jeffrey tried to make her feel guilty by accusing her of making him sick, she didn't take the bait. By making it clear that if he got sick it would be his own doing, Jeffrey's mother freed herself from a lot of needless nagging, pressuring, and reminding.

TEACHING PERSONAL RESPONSIBILITY

This brings us to another reason natural consequences work so well: *they make children take responsibility for their own actions.* If your children refuse to eat what you serve them, they have nobody to blame but themselves when they get hungry. If they burn their fingers on a hot pot after being warned once, they have no one to blame but themselves. And if they rock back on two legs of their chair and fall over backwards, they have nobody else to blame.

As long as you keep reminding your children, you make yourself responsible for their obedience. After all, why should they remember to be responsible for themselves when they know you will remind them? Once you stop, they have to decide whether they want to obey and act responsibly, or suffer the consequences. I know this is difficult. Nobody likes to see children suffer, particularly when it could have been prevented. Kathy and I felt miserable when Debbie got sick after eating soap. But the crucial point is this: You will never eliminate nagging and pressuring until you decide to let your children learn a few lessons the hard way.

TEACHING RESPECT FOR PARENTS

Natural consequences have one more advantage: *They teach children to respect you and to pay attention to your advice.* When Kathy and I told Debbie not to eat soap, but didn't force her to stop, she learned to take responsibility for not eating soap. She also learned that it wasn't a bad idea to listen to her mom and dad! She realized, "When my parents tell me not to do something, they are doing it for my good. Next time, I'd better pay attention."

Some parents think that the best way to teach children to respect them is to use their superior size to compel obedience. There are times for that—especially when children are about to do something that could severely harm them or someone else. But if you force your children too much they will start resenting you, and you will create unnecessary power struggles. Besides that, children who obey their parents only because they fear their superior power or their stern authority never learn to think for themselves, or to respect their parents' wisdom. It's one thing to obey someone because they are bigger than you. It's another thing to obey because you have learned to respect their wisdom and good judgment.

Children need to learn this lesson early, before they can make major life-destroying decisions. Wouldn't you rather have your children learn to respect your counsel by touching a hot stove or getting sunburned, than by becoming sexually involved before marriage or experimenting with drugs? If you allow your children to experience some painful lessons when they are young, when they hit adolescence they will be much less likely to reject your guidance. They will have learned, "When I go against my parents' advice, things usually go wrong. I think I'll listen."

Now let's see how natural consequences can work with two common problems: the forgetful child and the finicky eater.

THE FORGETFUL CHILD

Six-year-old Brittany kept forgetting to take her lunch to school. If her mother didn't hand it to her as she headed out the door, Brittany forgot. At lunchtime she would phone home frantically, and her mother would drop whatever she was doing to drive her daughter's lunch to school.

When Brittany's mother finally got tired of that routine, she asked me what to do. I told her about the principle of natural consequences, and she decided to try it. She sat down with Brittany and said, "Mother has a lot of work to do, and it is hard to interrupt it to bring your lunch to school. Besides that, you are in first grade now and Mother knows you are a big enough girl to remember your lunch." Then she told Brittany, "If you forget your lunch, you will have to go without—Mom won't bring it to you anymore."

Brittany protested, but seemed to get the message. The first few days went fine. But Thursday morning Brittany was in a hurry and forgot her lunch. She called her mother in a panic, but was gently and firmly reminded of their new arrangement. Brittany started crying, and her mother almost gave in. But she knew that if she didn't hold firm, she would be rewarding Brittany's forgetfulness and taking her lunch to school for years. So she told Brittany she was really sorry, but she would not bring her lunch. Brittany was in tears as she hung up. To Brittany's credit, she was a very creative girl; when she got off the phone, she talked a friend into sharing her lunch. But it was a long time before Brittany forgot again, and when she did, she didn't bother calling her mom. She took responsibility for herself.

Brittany's mom actually applied two training tools. She stopped rewarding Brittany's forgetfulness by bringing her lunch, and she used the natural consequence of letting Brittany go hungry. Together, they made Brittany a more responsible child. They also made life easier for her mother.

THE FINICKY EATER

Most families have at least one finicky eater, and in the Herrick's household it was Cody. Cody's parents tried everything they knew of to get him to eat. They put a small helping of mashed potatoes, meat, and peas on his plate and Cody just looked at it. They told him, "You want to grow up and be a big boy, don't you?" and he'd eat a bite or two and then stop. They tried to bribe him by saying, "If you eat your food, you can have dessert." Cody would eat a little more, but then start making rivers with his mashed potatoes and gravy.

They told him, "Hurry up, or you can't have any dessert." He said, "I don't want any dessert." So they finally gave up and sent him on his way.

Did you notice how Cody sucked his parents into a power struggle? Before they tried to make him eat, the problem was solely his. If he didn't like the food or didn't eat, he would suffer the consequence of going hungry. But instead of letting it go at that, his mom and dad decided it was *their* responsibility to make him eat. That started a power struggle. In so many words they told him, "You are a weak little child. We know what's best for you. Let us help you eat, and you can become a big boy." Cody unconsciously thought, *I'll show you who is a big boy now! I won't do what you say!* And the struggle was on. But it was all unnecessary.

What is the natural consequence of not eating? It's going hungry. A long time before God gave children mothers and fathers, he created the hunger pang button. We know that, because Adam and Eve didn't have parents telling them when to eat, and they got along just fine! The way to help children develop proper eating habits is to put reasonably attractive meals on the table, not let them snack between meals unless they ate the last meal, and let nature run its course. If they don't want to eat what you have prepared, simply remove all food from the table when you finish eating and inform them there will be no eating until the next meal.

In a couple of hours most children will ask for a bowl of cereal. If you don't let them snack, they will soon be so hungry they will eat anything you put on the table the next meal—even green beans and meat loaf! They won't need to be reminded, bribed, threatened, pressured, or rewarded. You don't see children in famine-riddled countries rejecting the food their parents set before them! Once children are hungry enough, they will eat what you give them.

You have a duty to provide healthy, reasonably tasty food for your children. But remember that children have different metabolic rates and different physical needs. Some children really don't need much to eat. At certain ages you shouldn't expect your children to like vegetables and foods made with gooey things like mayonnaise and sauces!

At other stages all some children may want to eat is cold cereal. If you are a member of the "one bite of everything" school, that's okay, but research shows that even if children are left entirely on their own, they will still get all of their required daily nutrients. I personally believe it is better to take the pressure and tension out of mealtime by offering a reasonable meal and then leaving our children alone.

	ONIONS	PEAS	CORN	BEANS	TOMATOES	SPINACH
MIKE	HATES THEM	LIKES THEM	LIKES IT	HATES THEM	HATES THEM	LIKES IT
TIM	LIKES THEM	HATES THEM	LOVES IT	HATES THEM	LIKES THEM	LOVES IT
KATIE	LIKES THEM	LIKES THEM	HATES IT	HATES THEM	HATES THEM	HATES IT
LISA	HATES THEM	HATES THEM	TOLERATES IT	HATES THEM	GAGS ON THEM	HATES IT
NICK	ALLERGIC	HATES THEM	Allerg.	ALLERG.	HATES THEM	ALLERG.
WILLIE	THROWS THEM	TOLERATES THEM	THROWS IT	THROWS THEM	THROWS	THROWS

Fathers generally find it easier to rely on natural consequences than mothers when it comes to eating. "Let the kid starve" or "He'll eat when he's ready!" fathers insist. But most mothers think, *Oh, no. My poor baby isn't getting enough to eat*, afraid that by morning their child will look like a starving orphan. Mothers feel this way because in their minds food is a symbol of love. After all, how do mothers first show love to their children? By breast- or bottle-feeding. When children don't eat, mothers feel that their love offerings are being rejected.

The hardest part of letting a finicky eater go hungry isn't at mealtime. It's a few hours later, when your child starts to get something out of the refrigerator and you remind him, "I'm sorry, Son.

You know if you don't finish supper you can't eat anything until our next meal." "But Mom," he protests, "I'm starving." Or worse yet, he cries out from his bed in a weak, pleading voice, "Moooommy, my tummy hurts. Can't I please just have one glass of milk?"

That's enough to send most mothers on a guilt trip to outer space. They reason, "Oh, no. I'm so cruel. Surely one glass of milk will be okay" or "Maybe just once won't hurt." But if you give in, you've had it. You are telling your son, "Just keep fussing and whining until Mother feels guilty. Then she will give in and protect you from the consequences of your own choices."

"But," you ask, "isn't it cruel to force a child to go to bed hungry?" Not at all. Remember, *you* are not *forcing* anybody to go to bed hungry. He is *choosing* to go to bed hungry. You are getting him to take responsibility for his actions. Going to bed hungry is the price your son pays for choosing not to eat. It doesn't take long for most children to decide that price is too high!

"But what about his health?" you ask. "We can't just let him starve." Oh, yes you can. Skipping a meal is not life-threatening. Besides that, remember that you aren't using natural consequences in order to deprive him of food. You are using natural consequences to teach him to eat better. If you can tolerate a little guilt as he misses a few meals, you will be on your way to years of peace at mealtime.

GUILT: YOUR CHILD'S BEST WEAPON

Why don't parents use natural consequences to let finicky eaters go hungry, forgetful children go without their school lunch, or inquisitive children touch hot objects? The answer is simple: guilt.

Children have conned parents into letting them evade more chores, homework, and last-minute projects by making them feel guilty than by any other tactic. Most children are so good at shifting the responsibility away from themselves, you may wonder if they were born with a dictionary of guilt-inducing comments. Do any of these sound familiar?

"I was too busy."
"Everyone else gets to go."
"But I'll starve."
"I'll miss the bus."

"I'm too tired."

"I'll get an F."

"My team needs me."

"I *never* get to do *anything*."

"I couldn't help it."

"*Bobby's* parents don't make *him*."

Since we parents make hundreds of decisions affecting our children each month, they have unparalleled opportunities to accuse us of being cruel and unreasonable. Knowing this, they quickly learn to use guilt to get us to do their bidding. It is absolutely crucial for you to learn to resist these efforts. It doesn't do one bit of good to know how to use natural consequences if you don't have the guts to let them do their work even though your children may yell, cry, or protest.

I recently counseled the wealthy parents of an irresponsible young adult. He refused to take a steady job and started one bad business venture after another. Instead of letting him feel the pain of poverty, his parents "helped" him out by giving him money to start business after business. Were they really helping? Not at all. Their good intentions actually compounded their son's problem by helping him avoid the painful consequences of his bad choices. They actually rewarded his failed efforts with more money!

What the son needed to hear was, "We love you, and we feel very badly that your business failed. We would like to help you start another one, but we are afraid the same thing might happen again. If the bank will loan you money for your next project, that's great, but we aren't ready to take another chance. If the bank won't loan you money, then maybe you will need to get a regular job, save up for a few years, and then try again." Faced with this response, the son may protest and assure his parents he has learned his lesson. But that's exactly what he said when he was a child: "I'll do better next time."

It is important to support our children when they fail, but we should not keep protecting them from the school of hard knocks. Only one thing would teach this aspiring business tycoon a lesson—failing, and suffering the consequences. As hard as that is for parents to watch, sometimes we have to let our children suffer pain so that they will become responsible in the future.

HOLDING FIRM

Once you get the hang of it, it's not that difficult to get your children to stop manipulating you with guilt; all it takes is some courage and five simple steps. First, make it clear to your children ahead of time that you are no longer going to bail them out if they don't meet their responsibilities. Tell them you have confidence that they can remember whatever it is they have to remember. Second, remind them briefly of the consequence of not following through. If they forget their lunch, they will have to do without. Third, get out of the way and let the consequences work. If they go hungry or get sunburned, let them suffer the consequences. Fourth, be sympathetic. Don't tell your children, "I told you so." Tell them, "I'm really sorry, honey." Finally, when they start crying or blaming you, remain firm, but loving. Tell them, "I really feel bad, honey, but this was our arrangement. We have tried other things and they didn't work. I know it's hard, but I'm sure you will remember next time."

RECAP

Many of your children's misbehaviors have built-in painful consequences. As long as the consequences won't cause severe or lasting damage, you can use them to train your children. Instead of pressuring your sons and daughters to obey you, you can teach them to take responsibility for their own actions by letting them suffer the natural consequences of their own decisions. In the process, you avoid unnecessary power struggles and they learn to respect your advice.

Of course there are times when natural consequences aren't appropriate. God has placed you in a position of responsibility and sometimes you need to directly intervene and discipline your children.[5] You will need more than natural consequences, for example, to see to it that your children clean their rooms or get along with their siblings. But you don't need to keep pressuring them or warning them about things having to do with their own possessions and their own bodies.

Now that you see how natural consequences work, we'll take a look in the next chapter at an equally powerful disciplinary tool called *logical consequences*.

Notes

1. R. Dreikurs and Gray, *Logical Consequences: A New Approach to Discipline* (Hawthorne, 1968).

2. Jeremiah 2:19.

3. Galatians 6:7.

4. Luke 15:11–24.

5. Ephesians 6:1.

CHAPTER 7

Logical Consequences: You *Can* Teach Children to Obey

Do you have trouble getting your children to clean their rooms, make their beds, do their chores, finish their homework, and stop fighting? If so, this chapter is for you. This chapter is also for you if you keep letting your children get by with the two favorite excuses of children around the world—"I couldn't hear you" and "I forgot."

Ask your son why he is late to supper, and he will probably tell you, "I was at Taylor's house and couldn't hear you call." Ask him why he didn't feed the dog, and he'll say, "I forgot." It's amazing how otherwise intelligent children with acute hearing suddenly become intellectually dull and deaf when asked to do things they don't want to do. But try whispering about a birthday present or talking confidentially with your mate, and children can hear every word from the other end of the house! Humorist Dave Barry describes what it takes to get his son to put on his shoes:

> If I want to make sure he has his shoes on by Monday morning, I have to start reminding him no later than Saturday afternoon. "Robert," I'll say, while he is engaged in some vital activity such as pouring PurpleSaurus Rex flavor Kool-Aid on the patio to form a Liquefied Sugar Theme Park for ants, "I want you to put on your shoes *right now*."
>
> "Okay," he'll say, with total sincerity. Meanwhile, inside his skull, a small but powerful organ found in children and known to medical science as the Instruction Diverter has taken my words as they entered his left ear and, before they could

begin to penetrate his brain, ejected them out his right ear at nearly the speed of light. He continues to stare at the ants. "What did I just ask you?" I'll ask.

"What?" he'll answer. He has *no idea* what we're talking about. At that very moment my instructions are whizzing past the asteroid belt.[1]

Have you ever stopped to think about these lapses of hearing and memory? They are really quite convenient. How can you discipline a deaf child or a child with a bad memory? It's not their fault. In fact, it's probably yours. If you had yelled louder or reminded him a few more times maybe he would have gotten the message. As twisted as this logic is, most parents fall for it. After all, we don't want to be cruel. If our children don't remember, shouldn't we remind them "just once more"? And if they can't hear, shouldn't we yell a little louder or call a little longer? You can if you want, but I assure you it won't work. Your children will keep playing on your guilty parental instincts to avoid their responsibilities for the next twenty years.

This chapter shows you a guaranteed way to improve your children's hearing and memory. It is called *logical consequences*. It is a lot like natural consequences, but with one exception. In natural consequences, there is a *built-in* consequence. When you touch a hot stove, you get burned. When you don't eat, you become hungry. In logical consequences, there is no built-in painful consequence. Instead, we parents have to create an undesirable consequence that "logically" follows our children's misbehavior.

What would be a logical consequence, for example, for a seventeen-year-old who "forgets" to wash the family car? It would be not driving the car. A logical consequence for a teenager who fails to keep a curfew? It would be not going out—being grounded for a while. I'm sure you have already tried something like this. When your children left their things all over the house you may have threatened, "If you don't pick up your stuff, I am going to give it to the Salvation Army." Angry threats, however, don't work for long. With logical consequences, just sit down with your children ahead of time, help them understand what is expected of them, and let them know the consequence of not following through. Then calmly but firmly implement the consequence. Don't raise your voice, threaten, or remind. Simply carry out the consequence.

"IF . . . THEN"

Someone has called logical consequences the "If–Then" method of discipline, because you tell your children, "_If_ you do that, _then_ this will happen." Explain the consequence of a misbehavior once. Then stay out of the way and let them decide if they want to suffer that consequence.

Logical consequences are like natural consequences in that they _help eliminate power struggles_. Instead of reminding or nagging our children, we simply set the consequence and remove ourselves from the battleground. Our children will choose to obey or suffer the consequences.

Also like natural consequences, logical consequences _insure that our children take responsibility for their own behavior._ Since we no longer follow them around the house reminding them of what they are supposed to do, they must learn to pay attention the first time we speak. After all, isn't this the way the real world works? If you don't pay your telephone bill, the phone company gives you a couple of warnings and then yanks the cord. If you don't go to work, your boss replaces you with someone who will. Your children may as well learn these lessons now.

Logical consequences operate on three basic premises. First, nagging and reminding ultimately don't help children become responsible, because our reminders eliminate their need to remember for themselves. Second, children will change their behavior when they suffer painful or negative consequences. Third, reminders actually protect children from one of the major motivations to change—

suffering the painful consequences of their behavior. Let's see how this works with some common childish misbehaviors:

- in the car
- at the dinner table
- doing homework
- getting off to school
- cleaning up
- doing chores

BACKSEAT BEDLAM

You are driving your children to gymnastics or soccer practice. All is quiet for the first two minutes—too quiet. You hear wrestling, then teasing, then combat. You know from past experience that someone will wind up crying, but when you warn them to be careful, they assure you, "We're just playing." Sure enough, soon the tears are flowing. Turning around, you discipline the offender, pacify the victim, or tell them both to settle down.

Notice the cycle? Your children misbehave. You threaten, warn, or punish. They ignore you or stop for awhile, but before long are at it again. When things get really bad you discipline, punish, or threaten more harshly. Every time you get in the car the hassle recurs.

If you want to stop this cycle, try this: Before you get into the car next time, tell your children, "When you fight in the car, it bothers me. So if you fight, I will pull off to the side of the road and wait until you can get along better." Then begin your trip. If your children start fighting, don't say a word. Simply slow down and head for the right shoulder. That maneuver is usually enough to bring a chorus of "We're sorry. We'll be quiet." If it isn't, go ahead and stop and wait for them to settle down.

You may think, "I'm the parent. I shouldn't have to be inconvenienced by stopping for screaming kids. Let them shape up." And in a way you are right. But remember, children have to be taught to get along, and this is one technique that works in a hurry. Children don't want to be late for their activities. Besides, wouldn't you be happy to trade the temporary inconvenience of pulling off the road a few times for ten or fifteen years of peaceful driving?

Chances are you have already threatened, "If you don't shape up, I'll turn this car around and take you straight home!" But that has two problems. First, you probably don't have the guts to follow through with your threat. Second, it's done in anger. Even if your children stop fighting, they are motivated more by your anger than by wanting to avoid the logical consequence of their misbehavior. It's better to tell your children the consequence ahead of time and calmly carry it out than to make angry or empty threats.

THE EVENING ROUNDUP

Here's another common hassle: getting everyone to the dinner table on time. Connie and Dan had a rough time rounding up their children for supper. Connie would start calling around 5:30 to get them to the table by 6:00. She would phone the neighbors to see if one of her children was there or yell at the top of her lungs to be sure the children could hear. After several years of this, Connie and Dan learned the principle of logical consequences. They asked themselves, "What would be the logical consequence of not arriving for supper on time?" The answer was obvious: no supper.

Connie and Dan hesitated to use such a drastic measure but they were tired of playing "detective" to find their children every evening, so they went ahead. They told their children they didn't want to look all over the neighborhood and call repeatedly every night. The children were old enough to take responsibility for making it to supper on time. Mother would call once, five minutes before supper. Anyone who was not in place by the time they finished praying would have to do without until the next meal.

The first night everyone was there. They just wanted to see what Mom and Dad were up to. The next night Mark was at a neighbor's and came in several minutes late. Connie felt a twinge of guilt at the thought of denying a meal to her hungry child and hesitated. She wanted to tell him, "Okay, you can eat tonight. But this is the last time." Since she had tried that before and it didn't work, she steeled herself and told Mark, "I'm sorry, Son, but you remember our rule. If you don't make it to supper on time, you can't eat until the next meal."

"But, Mom!" Mark appealed to his mother's guilt, "I couldn't hear you holler." Connie and Dan felt like giving in. Maybe they were being too tough. But then they remembered the alternatives. Mark either had to take responsibility for his lateness or they would have to call and nag him every day for the next ten years. That settled it! Dan supported his wife and told Mark, "You know our rule, Son. I'm sorry you are late. Next time you will need to watch the clock more closely." Dan didn't tell him, "I told you so," and he didn't try to rub it in. He simply stated the facts. Mark muttered something under his breath, left the table, went into his room, and slammed the door. Connie and Dan felt bad for a while, but their firmness paid off immediately. It was a long time before Mark was late again, and when he was, he took it in stride and didn't blame anyone else.

Notice how this worked. Before Connie and Dan started using logical consequences, *they* were taking responsibility away from their children. When Mark was late, *they* called him repeatedly or let him eat whenever he showed up. That reinforced Mark's tardiness and forgetfulness. Once they set up a consequence, the responsibility shifted to their children. If the children didn't want to eat, it wasn't Connie and Dan's problem. It was the children's. This eliminated Connie and Dan's need to become angry and frustrated. Since they now knew it wasn't their responsibility to get the children to the table, they didn't feel angry if the kids didn't show up. They didn't see their children as resisting them, being bad, or refusing to come. They simply saw them as choosing not to eat. The power struggle was dissolved.

If you think it isn't fair to have your children miss dinner, think of what would happen if you arrived at your favorite restaurant five minutes after closing time. Would you knock at the door, pleading, "Please let us in; we couldn't hear you holler"? I doubt it. And if you did, the manager wouldn't budge. He would kindly but firmly tell you, "I'm sorry, but we're closed." The next time you wanted to eat at that restaurant you would be sure to arrive a little before closing time. You wouldn't need another reminder.

Some parents handle missed suppers a little differently. They decide they shouldn't even have to call their children once. They set supper for a specific time. Anyone who isn't there, misses the meal.

Either of these options will work fine. The only requirement is a logical consequence that your children know they will suffer if they choose to be late.

If something completely unexpected and unavoidable makes it truly impossible for your children to be on time, don't be unreasonable and deny them dinner. But don't allow other exceptions or it won't work.

PROCRASTINATION

Eleven-year-old Amanda was a sixth-grader at the local elementary school. She was a bright child who did well in her studies, but she was a procrastinator. The night before a major paper was due was havoc. Amanda put off her big project for weeks, then expected her mom and dad to pull her out of the mess. Dad was sent downtown for art supplies, while mother and Amanda started writing. The clock passed nine, then ten, and then eleven. Even though it was well past her bedtime, Amanda anxiously told her mom, "I have to get it done if I stay up all night." Finally, around midnight, the report was finished. Everyone breathed a sigh of relief and headed for bed as Amanda promised this would never happen again. Everyone, of course, knew better. While her parents had threatened not to help Amanda, when it came down to the wire Amanda managed to get them to bail her out. How did she do it? Guilt!

When Amanda's parents first told her they wouldn't help her because she had procrastinated, Amanda had put on a frightened, upset look and told them, "But if I don't turn it in, I'll fail." At 11:00, when Amanda's parents said they had to go to bed, she began to cry. If her mom and dad left her with that forlorn, abandoned look, they would have felt incredibly guilty. So they stayed and worked another hour.

There is only one good way for Amanda to learn to stop procrastinating—logical consequences. Her parents need to tell her ahead of time that they will not help her if she waits until the last minute. Then they need to follow through the next time Amanda procrastinates. This may feel cruel, but it isn't. What is cruel is to let Amanda turn into a procrastinator who blames everyone else for her problems. A loving way to teach her to be responsible is to offer help with reasonable advance notice, and then to let her suffer the consequences if she procrastinates or "forgets."

THE OFF-TO-SCHOOL ROUTINE

Twelve-year-old Kristen was like a lot of children—she was a sleepy-eyed zombie in the morning. Kristen typically dragged herself out of bed fifteen or twenty minutes after her alarm went off, staggered into the bathroom half asleep, had to be called to the breakfast table, and barely caught the bus on time. About once a week she missed the bus, and would frantically run into the house with her first alert look of the day and yell, "Mom, you'll have to take me to school; I missed the bus!" Although Kristen's mom was furious, she didn't think she had another choice. So she would go to the garage, warm up the family car, and chauffeur Kristen to school.

Sound familiar? If it does, there's hope. Once Kristen's mom understood the concept of logical consequences, she realized her rescuing Kristen was part of the problem. Of course Kristen had a hard time getting up. Some children are just born that way. But her mom realized that every time she drove Kristen to school she was actually teaching her daughter, "It's fine to get up late, take your time in the bathroom, pick your way through breakfast, and miss the bus. *Mother* will solve your problem. *Mother* will take you to school. In fact, *Mother* will even start the car, warm it up for you, and give you some individual attention on the way."

What child in her right mind would pass up a deal like this? Kristen's mom was rewarding her daughter's sleepy-eyed style. Once she realized what was going on, Kristen's mom asked herself, *What are the consequences of not getting up on time, of not getting to breakfast, and of missing the bus?* The answers were simple. The consequence of being late for breakfast was not to eat until the next meal. And the logical consequence of missing the bus was walking to school, being late, or not going to school at all.

Kristen's mom sat down with her daughter and told her, "Kristen, mornings around here are too pressured. I know you have a hard time getting ready for school, but I realize I have been part of the problem. I've been worrying for you and pressuring you. When I drive you to school I'm really not helping you." She continued, "You are old enough to get yourself up and off to school without me nagging you, so I'm going to let you take charge of your mornings. I will fix breakfast and call you once if you want me to, but I won't call you two or three times, and I won't remind you or pressure you. I also won't drive you to school if you miss the bus. If you don't make it you will have to walk. I think if I get out of your way you can actually do better."

Sensing a dramatic change in her mother's attitude, Kristen immediately protested. "But Mom," she said, "it's too far to walk. I'll be late for class." "I know that, honey," her mom replied. "And that's why I'm sure you're going to find some way to make it on time." Sure enough, the next couple of mornings Kristen was punctual. But later that week she missed the bus again. When her mom wouldn't take her to school, Kristen begged and cried. Then she yelled, "You just don't care!" When she finally realized her mom wasn't giving in, she pulled out her last valiant effort and stubbornly pouted, "Then I'll just stay home," as she stamped into her room and slammed the door.

Before Kristen's mom understood how she was rewarding her daughter's slowness, she would have caved in and driven Kristen to school. This time she went into Kristen's room and said, "That's your choice, honey. If you leave now you can still make it in time for most of your first period, but if you would rather miss the whole day, that's up to you." About a half hour later Kristen headed off to school. She only missed the bus a couple of times after that.

Notice how Kristen's mom shifted the responsibility for being on time to Kristen. She said, "I have been worrying, I have been pressuring you, and I have been driving you to school. From now on I am going to remove myself and let you work it out." That is exactly what Kristen needed.

I realize the thought of letting your child miss school or arrive late may shock you. You may think, "What if there is a big exam and missing it would ruin her grade?" or "What if the principal finds out that my perfectly healthy child missed a day of school because I wouldn't drive her?"

But remember, it's not your fault that your child misses the bus or a day of school. If you think the teacher or principal will be upset, phone the school, tell them your problem and how you plan to solve it. Most teachers are thrilled to see a parent take charge like this. If your teacher happens to get upset, your child will have to take that consequence. After all it is her fault, not yours. The displeasure of a teacher may do more to get your daughter to school on time than all your nagging! And for most children, missing school one day or walking to school will be enough to solve this sleepy-eyed routine. Keep your ultimate goal in mind. You are letting her miss school or be late a few times so she will become responsible in the future.

If you work and can't let your children stay home, you will need to come up with a different consequence—like no television or no play that evening. But whatever consequence you choose must be calmly and firmly carried out.

MESSY ROOMS

If your children leave a trail of junk from the family room to their bedrooms, you have probably tried everything to get them to pick it up. You may have shamed your son with comments like, "Look at that mess. A pig would feel uncomfortable in there." You might have threatened, "If somebody trips on your skateboard and breaks a leg, I'm not going to pay the bill." Or you may have tried guilt: "I pick up after your *father*, and I pick up after your *sister*. At least *you* could make my life a little easier."

These tactics don't work because they all depend on you. Just like getting children to the dinner table by calling repeatedly, *you* have to remind your children. *You* have to threaten them if they don't follow through. And even if your children finally pick up their things, they have done it because *you* nagged them, not because *they* learned to be responsible.

Here is a better way. Start a "Saturday box." A Saturday box is a large box that you put in a locked room or on a high shelf. Sit down with your children and tell them, "Mom is getting tired of picking up after everybody. My back is hurting and I'm getting too old to do this anymore. I get upset when I keep reminding you to pick up your things, and I suppose you don't like my nagging you either, so we are going to set a certain time of day that all the public rooms of the house are to be picked up. At that time each day I will go through the house. Anything that isn't in its place will be put in a box and can't be retrieved until Saturday. We'll call the box the Saturday box to remind us that if we leave our things out, we won't get to use them until Saturday."

Answer any questions or complaints your children have, agree on the time of day things are to be picked up, and then sit back and wait. The first day or so they probably won't leave out anything important. But about Wednesday or Thursday your son is likely to come to you asking, "Mom, where is my green sweater?" or "Where is my soccer ball?" You reply, "I'm not sure, Son, but I think I remember putting it in the Saturday box." With the most innocent look in the world he will reply, "Well, will you get it for me, Mom? I have to have it for school today."

That's when your struggle begins. When you remind him of your new rule he will protest, "But Mom, I *have* to have it. It's the only ball the team has." "I'm really sorry, Son," you reply, "but you know you can't have it back until Saturday."

At this point your son will probably throw a tantrum. He may say, "I'll look like a jerk, and it will be your fault!" or "Our whole team won't get to practice, and it will be your fault!" Don't fall for his guilt trip. *It is not your fault.* He is trying to make you feel guilty so he can avoid facing his own irresponsibility. Be sympathetic. If you have to, bite your lip to keep from saying, "I told you so." And don't give in. Remember, he chose (consciously or unconsciously) to leave his ball out, assuming that you wouldn't hold him responsible. The only thing that will motivate him to pick up his stuff next time is the knowledge that he will pay a price if he doesn't.

The Saturday box will work for any room in the house, but you may decide not to apply it to all of them. Certainly, children shouldn't leave stuff in the living room or hallway, but if your child has his own room, you might let him decide how neat he wants that room to be. You might require him to make the bed and have at least a little order, but most parents don't require their children to keep their rooms completely neat and orderly. Once you have decided what rooms have to be picked up, however, the Saturday box is a great way to see that your children comply.

Now that you have these steps down, let's see how they work with two more common problems—a noisy, impolite child at the dinner table, and a child who misbehaves at school or around the house.

MEALTIME MADNESS

Derek, a noisy eight-year-old who was impolite and teased his sisters, kept up a continuous, one-sided chatter during meals. His parents brought him to a psychologist for counseling. After studying the entire family situation the psychologist suggested that the parents isolate Derek during mealtimes if he couldn't get along. She suggested that Mother set up a card table in another room and allow Derek to eat by himself. He would be told, "We love you and would like you to be with us, but we need to relax at mealtime. When you can be quiet, you may eat with us. Until then, you must eat by yourself."

The minute the psychologist laid out her proposal Derek's mother protested. "That would be rejecting him," she said. "Not at all!" the psychologist replied. "You aren't telling Derek, 'We don't like you. You must eat by yourself.' You are telling him you love him and want him to eat with you in a way you can all enjoy, but that if he acts up, he will be choosing to eat by himself. If he says, 'You hate me!' just tell him, 'No, Son. We really love you and want you to be with us. But we also need a quiet time for supper. As soon as you can get along you will eat with us again.'"

The psychologist also helped Derek's parents see that they had two problems. One was Derek's obnoxious behavior; the other was his poor feelings about himself. Derek's acting up was his way of saying "I don't feel good about myself." Because of this, isolating him at meals wouldn't solve the underlying problem. But while Derek's parents and therapist were helping him with the underlying problem, helping him get along with others at meals gave the family some peace and also helped Derek learn better social skills.

Notice also how the logical consequences of eating alone brought a stop to the rewards (attention) Derek had been getting for acting up at the dinner table. When Derek was able to sit relatively quietly with his family, he received the reward of being with them.

THE TIME-OUT TECHNIQUE

Many teachers use a consequence like Derek's parents under the label of a "time-out" technique. They simply tell their students, "If you talk out of turn you will have to go to the time-out room or sit by yourself in the back of the room." The time-out technique is different from the old dunce cap and chair because those methods shamed children and gave them a great chance to get attention for their misbehaviors. In time-out we simply remove them from view so they can't gain attention by acting up in front of their classmates.

If you decide to use the time-out technique at home, select a spot in the house to send your child. Try to pick a quiet, boring place close enough that you can observe, since you don't want your children to be able to entertain themselves. The hallway or a corner of the living room generally makes a good location. You may also need to buy an egg timer. If your child gets out of his chair, simply reset the timer. But be careful about two things in using time-outs: Don't use it when you are angry, and set definite limits. If you get mad and send your child to his room to punish him or get even, it won't work. He will know you are still in a power struggle and are punishing him, and he will have a sense of satisfaction for upsetting you. That may be a big enough reward to encourage him to do it again.

Second, time-outs should have definite limits. Five minutes is usually a good beginning time. After the next offense the time may be lengthened to ten minutes. It doesn't take most children long to learn it is better to behave and enjoy their family and friends than to misbehave and spend a half hour by themselves!

DEVELOPING A PLAN

By now you can see how well logical consequences work. But let's spell out the specific steps you need to take to implement them before we go on to our final techniques of discipline. Begin by identifying the problem with your children. Call a family meeting and explain, "I am getting tired of calling you several times to come to supper (or reminding you to do your chores, or practice the piano). You probably don't like my nagging you either." Then tell them you want to find a way to get them to remember their jobs without nagging and reminding. You might say, "We've got to think of some way of getting you to do your jobs without my hassling you" or, "We will have to decide on something that will automatically happen each time you forget your chores (or don't come when I call) in order to help you remember next time."

Once you have introduced the plan, ask your children if they have any ideas that would help them remember. Some children get the idea right away and say, "If I forget to wash the car, I can't drive it that weekend" or, "If I don't feed the dog, we will have to give him away." If they come up with a good idea, great. Agree with them and move ahead.

If your children have trouble thinking of an appropriate consequence, or if they simply promise you they will do better next time, tell them, "I'm sorry, honey, but I don't think that will work. We've tried that before but you keep forgetting." Then come up with your own consequence. Tell them, "Unless you can think of a better one, I think it's fair that if you don't make it to supper on time you don't eat that night (or if you don't mow the yard Saturday morning, you can't go to your baseball game until the yard is finished)."

If your children do what they are supposed to, great. Your problem is solved. If not, you simply carry out the predetermined consequence. Don't remind them and don't get angry and threaten them. Simply tell them, "I'm sorry, but you know the rules. You can't go to your game until the yard is mowed." Then take a deep breath and with all the grit, backbone, and dogged determination you can muster, stand firm against their inevitable efforts to get you to cave in and return to the old way. Each time they come up with another excuse tell them, "I'm sorry but we discussed this last week and you knew this is what would happen if you didn't finish the job" or, "I'm really sorry, but the longer you wait, the later you will be to your game."

Notice several things about using logical consequences. First, you don't wait until your children "forget." You sit down with them ahead of time, talk over the problem, and let them know the consequence. Second, since you aren't in the heat of a conflict, it's easier to keep calm and discipline lovingly but firmly instead of punishing out of anger. Third, you leave it up to your children to take responsibility for their choices. You don't bail them out by reminding them or giving in and doing it yourself. And finally, you don't let them manipulate you because they've made you feel guilty.

RECAP

Logical consequences is the fifth technique of discipline. It works because experience really is the best teacher. Logical consequences also remove us from power struggles and teach children to take responsibility for their own behavior.

In addition to the problems we've already discussed, you can use logical consequences to see that your children do almost any chore around the house. If you have trouble getting your children to feed their pet, for example, you have two choices: either give the pet away or, assuming you have become attached to the pet, simply tell your child, "We each have responsibilities around the house. I feed the people, and you feed the animals. If you forget to feed the dog, then I won't feed you."

If your child doesn't practice the piano, you can simply say, "If you don't practice, I won't pay for lessons." Or, if you are convinced your child has talent, but needs more motivation, "As soon as you finish practicing the piano each day, you can watch TV or go out to play." If your son leaves his six-week term paper in the middle of the living room, handle it like everything else that is left out. Put it in the Saturday box.

These consequences may sound severe at first, but remember your attitude and your motives, and the way you present them. You are not trying to punish your children or hurt them. Your are disciplining them by making sure they take responsibility for their actions.

Notes

1. Dave Barry, *Dave Barry Turns 40* (New York: Fawcett, 1991), 66.

CHAPTER 8

To Spank or Not to Spank?

Several years ago I received a phone call from the program chairperson for the National Association for the Prevention of Child Abuse. She was looking for a psychologist to debate the organization's president at their upcoming national conference. The topic to be debated was, "Is all physical discipline child abuse?" Their president believed it was, and they were having a tough time finding a psychologist who would take the opposing side and advocate the use of good old-fashioned spankings. I took up the challenge.

The president and I staked out our positions in front of about two thousand social workers, psychologists, psychiatrists, and other professional and lay workers. She argued that many parents severely abuse children through spanking, that spankings don't work, that they are cruel, that they give children models of how to solve problems with violence, and that they are a remnant of our unsophisticated past and no longer necessary in our enlightened age.

I agreed that many parents abuse children under the guise of spanking, but I also argued that physical correction doesn't have to be abusive. I reminded my colleague that children can be equally abused emotionally through verbal blows like "stupid," "clumsy," and "idiot." Then I pointed out that there is a difference between firmly but calmly giving a child a swat and hitting a child in anger. And I added that young children don't have the abstract reasoning ability to understand more sophisticated, verbal forms of discipline. Young children think concretely. They understand a simple no and a spank on the hand or the bottom much better than a lengthy dialogue on the inappropriateness of their actions. You can't sit down and tell a fourteen-month-old, "Sweetheart, let's discuss the philosophical and psychological implications of throwing your toys at your sister."

When we finished our debate and turned off the microphone, my opponent turned to me and said, "I hadn't thought of it that way. You almost convinced me." Other conferees commented, "I've never thought about the possibility of spanking a child without being angry." One mentioned, "I'd never thought about the fact that preschool children have almost no abstract reasoning ability."

IS SPANKING CHILD ABUSE?

The professional mental health workers mentioned above had seen so much abuse and heard so many horror stories, that they unthinkingly accepted the argument that all spanking is abusive. I can understand their reasoning. In 1990, over two and a half million reports of child abuse were filed in the United States.[1] That's enough children to populate an entire city larger than Denver, Phoenix, or Atlanta every year! While some of those reports may be exaggerated, and others were for sexual and emotional abuse, the single largest number was for physical abuse. And many of those happened under the guise of physical punishment. By discouraging all spanking, social activists and health professionals hope to eliminate these cases of abuse. They also warn that since children learn by watching their parents, children who are spanked may learn to use physical violence to solve their own problems. It is a fact that children who are abused have a much greater likelihood of growing up to abuse their own children.

ABUSE IN CHRISTIAN CLOTHING

Several years ago I read a newspaper article about a Christian couple whose children had just been removed from their home because of excessive and severe corporal punishment from their parents.[2] The abuse came to light when the couple's twenty-year-old daughter ran away from home and told a counselor how her parents punished the children.

According to the police, the children were forced to expose their bare bottoms to be spanked with a thin bamboo stick every time they needed correction—which was often several times a day. Each correction was four or more whacks on the bare bottom, and police investigators said their backsides "looked like shoe leather" from repeated punishment.

The children were punished for even minor infractions of family rules, like wiggling during story time. The parents were supposedly following the teachings of two Christian authors who wrote:

> My obedience to God to train my child requires that every time I ask him to do something, whatever it is, I must see that he obeys. When I have said it once in a normal tone, if he does not obey immediately, I must take up the switch and correct him enough to hurt so he will not want it repeated.[3]

The authors go on to tell their readers that since some children are well-behaved they must be punished for small infractions in order to teach them obedience.

Another article told of an American evangelist who teaches parents to "break their will," "blister their bottom red," and to spank week-old babies. He tells listeners that girls might not need spanking until three weeks of age but boys will need to be punished physically from the time they are a few days old![4] Think of it: a minister of God recommending spanking a newborn infant! This is not only cruel and abusive, it's nonsense. Newborns aren't even aware that there is such a thing as right and wrong. All they know when they are hit is that they are living in a cruel world filled with pain instead of love and safety. Christian parents need to completely reject this abusive treatment of children. Never mind that misguided teachers use a Scripture verse or two wrenched out of context to support their position. This position is simply not biblical.

Unfortunately, these stories of Christian parents abusing children under the guise of discipline are not isolated instances. They reflect the real potential danger of physical discipline. Any time spanking is done out of parental anger, rather than love for the child, it is abusive. Go to any public place and watch parents with their children, and you will probably see one or more parents angrily grab their children or impulsively hit them. Other parents strike their children angrily or shake them when they can't get them to obey. Ten percent of child abuse cases come from severe shakes that have caused spinal cord and brain injuries. All angry corporal punishment frightens sensitive children and undermines their sense of safety, belonging, and security. In strong-willed or more rebellious children, it creates anger and the desire for revenge on the parent.

SHOULD WE SPARE THE ROD?

Opponents of spanking aren't all trying to undermine parental authority and let children run wild and do as they please. They have some valid concerns. Sometimes spankings don't work and the potential to abuse them should make all parents think seriously about the wisdom of spanking. Christian parents, especially, should be sensitive to the need to lovingly and patiently nurture children the way God, our heavenly Father, nurtures us. But does this mean we should never spank our children? Not at all. The fact that some parents abuse children with words doesn't mean we should never talk to our children, and the fact that some parents abuse children through spanking doesn't mean parents should never spank their children.

The Bible supports the occasional, restrained use of physical discipline. One proverb tells us, "He who spares the rod hates his son, but he who loves him is careful to discipline him."[5] This verse makes it clear there is a place for spanking, but it also tells us something about how to go about it. Like all good discipline, spankings should flow from love and be done for our children's welfare.

When our daughter was about a year of age, she started throwing her silverware on the floor. We would have liked to reason with Debbie, but she was too young to understand. If we used a logical consequence and took her food away, she wouldn't have seen the connection between throwing spoons and losing her food. She would have thought we were starving her for no reason. Since no other discipline would work, the next time Debbie threw a spoon on the floor we simply told her "No-no" and gave her a firm but non-angry spank on her hands. Within a week she went from throwing an average of five spoons on the floor each day to one. A couple of days later, she stopped entirely. We didn't damage Debbie or abuse her. We simply taught her to control her behavior by using the only discipline that would work. Like Debbie, most children can profit from a little physical discipline if it's done correctly.

The Bible mentions several types of discipline—instruction by words (Deut. 4:36), instruction from the heart (Ps. 16:7), instruction through the consequences of our actions (Luke 15:11–32), and spanking (Prov. 22:15). Spanking is only one method of discipline, and it should by no means be our major method of child training. Spankings are helpful only when they are used appropriately and in a good balance with other forms of discipline. Following are some specific guidelines to help you decide when a spanking is appropriate.

SPANK ONLY IF . . .

First, *never spank a child when you are angry*. Angry spankings are as unbiblical as failing to discipline. In fact, angry spankings aren't discipline—they're punishment. And they are abusive. By your example, they teach children that the only way to get someone else to control their behavior is to lose control of yours. God never corrects his children in anger, and we shouldn't, either. Remember the difference between punishment and discipline? Striking children in anger humiliates them, frightens them, and makes them angry or depressed. The Bible tells us "there is no fear in love,"[6] and that we shouldn't provoke our children to anger because that discourages them.[7] Just imagine how you would feel if someone two or three times your size got furious and hit you! That's how children feel when they are spanked by an angry parent.

I realize it is easier to *say* we shouldn't spank in anger than it is to actually avoid it. Most of us occasionally lose our tempers or have times when we feel furious and almost strike a child. If you have felt this way, you know the line between maintaining control and losing it can be a thin one. But hitting is not the answer. In chapter 10 I will show you how you can handle your anger so you can discipline your children more lovingly. In the meantime, I simply want to lay out this biblical principle: There are occasions for spanking children, but we should spank in love. We want our children to grow and learn through discipline, not because we are upset and angry.

Here is a second guideline for physical discipline: *Be sure the discipline is appropriate to the age of your child*. During most of the first year of life children cannot comprehend the meaning of a spanking. Consequently, during those early months, it is cruel and abusive to spank. By the time children reach about a year of age their central nervous system has developed to the point that they can grasp the meaning of a no and a spank on the hand. Usually one or two spanks is the most physical discipline a child that age should receive. Any more is punitive and abusive.

From about a year of age until they turn three or four is probably the most appropriate time for physical discipline. During those years it's difficult to reason with a child and there aren't always good logical consequences. Spanking should not be your primary discipline during this period, but it does have a place. Probably the best way to handle most of your toddler's misbehaviors is to distract him, kiddie-proof your home, remove him from the scene of the crime, or get him involved in interesting activities. You can also use the time-out technique we discussed in chapter 7. If you are spanking frequently, that probably means you haven't found more effective forms of discipline or some good preventive actions.

By the time children reach school age they respond better to reasoning and appropriate logical consequences than they do to spanking. They learn their lessons much better if they suffer logical consequences like missing a meal, forfeiting their favorite television program, or losing play time with a friend.

Spanking teenagers is a sure sign that you have lost control and that your relationship is crumbling. There are always better ways of disciplining teenagers than to humiliate and infuriate them by spanking them.

This leads to my third guideline: *Don't utilize physical spankings when there is another equally or more effective means of discipline.* I recommend this because spankings can be so easily abused. Parents generally hit their children because they feel frustrated and don't know what else to do. Don't fall into this trap. This book describes many other loving, sensitive, and successful ways of dealing with behavior problems.

Finally, remember that *spankings don't solve the underlying problem.* If your children are misbehaving because they feel unloved, incompetent, worthless, or bored, a spanking may temporarily stop the symptom, but it won't solve the real problem—one or more of their basic unmet emotional needs. Effective discipline must include ways of addressing these inner needs and the sources of their problems before they turn into misbehaviors.

That is why some parents have reared healthy, disciplined children with minimal or no spanking at all. They were sensitive to their children's needs, helped them feel loved, confident, and valuable, and corrected them with appropriate loving consequences instead of spanking. I am not recommending you never spank, but I strongly urge you to never spank in anger and to always ask yourself if there is a more effective way.

RECAP

Physical discipline can be an important part of rearing young children as long as you remember these guidelines:

- Never spank a child in anger.
- Other methods of discipline are equally or more appropriate for most situations.
- If your child is looking for attention or trying to gain revenge by upsetting you, spankings won't work. They may actually reward his misbehavior.
- The age of your child and the options of using natural and logical consequences can help you determine when you should spank and when you should not.
- From about age one until four is the most appropriate time for spankings.
- Spankings don't help meet your children's hidden emotional needs, which cause much of their misbehavior. Effectiveness of spanking is, therefore, limited to temporarily controlling behavior, not helping children feel understood or enabling them to grow emotionally.

Notes

1. The *Orange County Register*, 9 February 1992.
2. *San Jose Mercury News*, 19 February 1983.
3. Al Fabrijio and Pat Fabrijio, *Children: Fun or Frenzy?* (Palo Alto, CA: Alegri Press, 1969), 10.

4. The *Stars and Stripes*, 26 July 1992.
5. Proverbs 13:24.
6. 1 John 4:18.
7. Colossians 3:21.

CHAPTER 9

Creating a Plan and Making It Work

We have discussed six techniques or ways to discipline your children:

- extinction
- reinforcement or reward
- modeling
- natural consequence
- logical consequence
- spanking

Now we come to the crucial point—putting them in action. This chapter will show you how to develop and implement a step-by-step discipline plan for addressing any type of misbehavior. Sometimes the plan will be as simple as not passing the fried chicken (a reward) until your son says please. Sometimes it is as simple as letting your daughter refuse to eat and suffer the natural consequence of hunger. And sometimes it will mean getting your sixteen-year-old to wash the car by implementing this logical consequence: if the car isn't washed by an agreed-upon day and time, he doesn't use it that week. Other times, finding the solution will take more effort and creativity. When that is the case, you may have to sit down and carefully think through your strategy.

STEP ONE: IDENTIFY THE PROBLEM

No discipline works until we and our children are clear about the problem we want to solve. Don't tell your children, "I want you to get along with each other and cooperate more." That's too general. Broad, general problems are impossible to solve. Start by breaking a big problem into several smaller ones. Identify specific misbehaviors like, "I don't want to have to call you several times to get you out of bed in the morning" or "I want you and Bill to stop fighting" or "I want you to clean your room without being reminded."

Once you identify the problems, pick one to start with, and don't make it the biggest one. Work on a couple of small to medium-size problems until you and your children get the hang of it. Then you can move on to the bigger ones.

And remember to pick your battles. Kids will be kids, and our goal isn't to turn them into miniature adults. Ignore some little problems and only discipline for things that really matter. Otherwise you will be disciplining your children so often that they will start resenting you and losing the fun of life.

STEP TWO: TAKE PREVENTIVE ACTION

Before you implement any corrective disciplines, take two preventive steps. First, be sure you have done all you can to train them to do what you expect. Take, for example, getting off to school in the mornings. Before you let your daughter suffer the consequence of missing the school bus, help her plan her mornings step by step. Figure out how long it takes her to wake up, bathe, dress, eat breakfast, and practice the piano. Then work back from the time she needs to meet the bus to determine the time she should get up. You might also develop a "job box" or "chore chart" that lists everything she needs to do each morning. Put it on the refrigerator door or some other conspicuous place, and tell her that before breakfast she must take the slips of paper for each morning activity and move them from the "To Do" slot to the "Done" slot. Never forget that children need this kind of step-by-step planning to meet their deadlines and responsibilities. When you and I have a bus to catch, we just naturally think back from that deadline and arrange to do our jobs in time. Most children don't. They need us to train them and show them how to do even simple planning. Having a job chart also gets you out of nagging, since the "chore chart" or "job box" does the reminding for you.

The same thing goes for any new task. Don't just tell your son to mow the yard. Do it with him a couple of times. Show him how to start the mower, how to fill it with gas, and where or how to pile the clippings, and how to put things away. Once he knows the steps well, then you can let him suffer the consequences if he fails to follow through.

The second preventive step is to understand *why* they are misbehaving, so you can fix the real problem. In chapter 2 we saw that children generally misbehave because they are trying to meet their God-given needs for love, confidence, worth, or constructive activity by turning to the substitutes of attention, power, or destructive activity. They also misbehave because, like all of us, they have a selfish desire to do things their own way. Or they may be looking for revenge or psychological safety. Any of these motives can set your children's misbehavior in motion.

Once you know what is causing your child's behavior problem, you may be able to solve it without any corrective discipline. When our son was just a toddler, we had a beautiful cloisonné vase from China on our living room coffee table. Richard was interested in this vase and in spite of our warnings and spanks on the hand, he kept touching it. Finally, we wised up and put the vase on a high shelf in another part of the house until Richard was a little older. That immediately solved our problem. The Bible says that God does not tempt us beyond what we can bear,[1] but we had been doing precisely that to Richard. It's unreasonable to expect toddlers to withstand the temptation to touch things that are within their reach. We prevented a bad situation by a simple preventive action.

Suppose your daughter is misbehaving in order to gain attention because you recently took a job or other responsibilities that cut into your time together. An appropriate logical consequence would be sending her to her room. That might temporarily change her behavior, but it won't fill her God-given need for love. Before you start corrective discipline, do everything you can to make her feel loved and included. Start by helping her feel better about herself. Spend more time with her. Listen to her struggles. Let her tell you how she feels about your being away. Once you have met her needs, she may stop misbehaving. If she doesn't, you can combine renewed efforts to meet her needs with a logical consequence, like having her spend some time in her room when she won't behave.

Sometimes just realizing that a problem is normal helps us to tolerate what we can't change. I am writing this chapter on a plane, and just in front of me is a patient dad with a crying eighteen-month-old son. The boy is tired, his ears are probably hurting, and he misses his mother. None of his dad's efforts to comfort him are working, but the dad isn't getting angry or spanking him. Instead, he is just trying to minimize the problem by waiting patiently until the plane lands or his son falls asleep. Understanding the causes of your child's actions can help you keep your sanity at times like this.

STEP THREE: ELIMINATE REWARDS FOR MISBEHAVIOR

Once you know what is causing your children to misbehave, ask yourself, "Are they getting a reward for misbehaving?" As soon as you find out how you have been rewarding your children's misbehavior, eliminate the rewards. You must remove the pleasures or rewards in order to increase their motivation to change.

"NOW WHAT HAVE I TOLD YOU? NEVER BOTHER MOMMY WHEN SHE'S IN THE BATHROOM!"

STEP FOUR: REWARD POSITIVE BEHAVIOR

At the same time you remove rewards for misbehavior, try to reward an opposite, desirable action. Children can't say "gimme" and "please" at the same time. So if you reward "please," you will be lessening the likelihood that your children will say "gimme."

Take teaching children to clean their rooms. Once you have shown them how you want it done, a simple "You did a great job" or "Your room looks great" encourages them and increases the likelihood of a repeat performance. You may need to couple this with a logical consequence like "You can't go out to play until your room is picked up," but a good reward is the best place to begin.

The same thing applies if your oldest daughter has a hard time getting along with her little sister. If she is especially nice one day, or puts up with a lot of her little sister's interruptions, take her out of earshot of her sister, give her a hug, and let her know that you know sometimes it's tough getting along with her sister. Tell her you would like to take her out for a special treat to thank her. When you reward her for getting along, you weaken her old habit of fighting.

Social rewards like compliments, hugs, and time together should always be a part of our training repertoire, and nonsocial rewards like stickers, money, candy, or special privileges may also have a place. Rewards are especially helpful when children are learning a new task or taking on a new responsibility. Rewards tell your children, "You're doing well; you can make it."

STEP FIVE: LET NATURE RUN ITS COURSE

Sometimes you won't need to go through any of these steps. You may immediately decide, *This is a normal childish action and all I need to do is let a natural consequence solve the problem.* As you have seen by now, natural consequences are especially effective on behaviors that impact your children's bodies (like not eating or not dressing warmly) or impact their possessions. If your children are about to do something that will cause nonfatal pain, or that will only harm their own possessions, warn them once and then keep quiet. Once they feel some pain, their own healthy self-interest will make them choose not to suffer that pain again.

Remember, it's better for children to suffer a little pain now than to be nagged and pressured for twenty years. And it's better for them to learn to trust your advice now instead of waiting until they are teenagers, when the stakes are higher: drinking and driving, using drugs, or engaging in premarital sex. The temporary pain of a natural consequence is nearly always more effective than all the warnings and other discipline you can muster. It is also a great way to teach children to respect your advice.

STEP SIX: ESTABLISH LOGICAL CONSEQUENCES

If meeting your children's needs, preventive training, extinction, rewards, and natural consequences don't do the trick, it's probably time for a logical consequence. Most children need a few painful consequences to go along with rewards, training, and good emotional nurturing in order to increase their motivation. Logical consequences is the discipline of choice when natural consequences don't exist or would cause severe or lasting damage.

Logical consequences work best after you have communicated what you expect your children to do and they haven't followed through. Start by telling your children exactly what you expect and precisely what consequences will follow if they don't obey. Then carry them out. Logical consequences are especially appropriate for children who keep "forgetting" their chores or who "can't hear." They work wonders on messy rooms, lateness, chores, homework, fighting, and failing to practice the piano or other instrument.

STEP SEVEN: PHYSICAL DISCIPLINE

Spankings or a spank on the hand accompanied by a "No-no" are appropriate when a child is at least a year of age, but still too young to profit from reasoning or other forms of discipline. Spanking may be the discipline of choice with young children when natural consequences would cause severe or lasting damage and when the child is too young to understand a logical consequence. Spanking is also appropriate when a young child cannot simply be removed from the scene of the crime. When Debbie was a year old and threw spoons on the floor at mealtime, we couldn't use the natural consequence of letting her go hungry or the logical consequence of not letting her eat because she wasn't old enough to understand. But our spank on the hand taught her a lesson.

Spankings may also work for children who keep getting into rooms or closets when they shouldn't. But be careful. Your first efforts should be to move the temptation out of reach, remove the child from that room, or come up with a logical consequence like, "If you break it, you will have to buy Mom another one." If none of those work for a toddler, a swat may be appropriate. If you do spank, however, remember never to spank in anger. Otherwise, your intended lesson will be lost behind your children's fear, anger, or discouragement.

CHOOSING THE BEST DISCIPLINE

Rarely does just one type of discipline work all by itself. Happy children who feel loved, confident, and valuable, and who have plenty of interesting activities to keep them occupied don't misbehave a lot. But they will still need at least a little corrective discipline. Rewards are great ways to encourage children to keep their rooms clean and to get along with each other. But most children will need some natural and logical consequences to heighten their motivation. And sometimes a firm but loving spanking may be an important part of your parental duty.

The following table lists the most appropriate times to use each form of discipline.

Table 1
CHOOSING A METHOD OF DISCIPLINE

Method of Discipline	When to Use	Lesson the Child Learns
REINFORCEMENT OR REWARDS	1. Anytime you want to strengthen a desirable behavior. 2. Especially helpful when learning new skills or taking new responsibilities.	"When I do the desirable thing, I get rewarded for it. Therefore, I will do it again."

Table 1 con't.

CHOOSING A METHOD OF DISCIPLINE

Method of Discipline	When to Use	Lesson the Child Learns
EXTINCTION/OR REMOVING REWARDS FOR MISBEHAVIOR	1. Anytime you want to weaken undesirable behavior. 2. Especially effective when combined with a reward for a competing positive behavior.	"When I behave undesirably, I do not get any reward. Therefore, there is no sense in doing that again."
IMITATION	This method is in continuous operation.	"My parents are strong and grown-up. Since they act that way, I want to be like them."
NATURAL CONSEQUENCES	1. When you want to weaken undesirable behavior. 2. When the act has a potentially painful result. 3. When children ignore your advice.	"When I do some things I get hurt. Nobody else has anything to do with it. I just bring on a bad experience. Therefore, I will not do that again. I also realize it's good to listen to my parents."
LOGICAL CONSEQUENCES	1. When you want to weaken undesirable behavior. 2. When no natural consequence exists. 3. When natural consequences would cause severe or lasting hurt to the child. 4. When you are being sucked into a power struggle.	"When I do something that is wrong, my parents or teachers may impose some undesirable consequences. Therefore, I will do my part in order to avoid the negative consequences."

Table 1 con't.

CHOOSING A METHOD OF DISCIPLINE

Method of Discipline	When to Use	Lesson the Child Learns
PHYSICAL SPANKING	1. When children are at least a year of age but still too young to profit from other disciplines. 2. When we can do it lovingly. 3. Where there is no other appropriate consequence.	"My parents are my authority. They have the experience to know what is right and to enforce their guidelines by inflicting physical pain. Though I do not like it at the time, I am learning it is for my good and they do it because they love me."

RECAP

Effective discipline begins by understanding and being sensitive to our children's needs and feelings. Once we emotionally put ourselves in our children's shoes, we can select the proper discipline. The cause of the problem, our children's ages, and their own personalities should influence our choice of disciplinary methods. Chapter 14, which discusses five of the most common questions parents ask, will give you more suggestions on how to implement these disciplinary tools.

Note

1. 1 Corinthians 10:13.

CHAPTER 10

Keeping Your Cool While Your Children Are Losing Theirs

Twelve-year-old Chad sassed his mother just as his dad walked into the house from work. In a fit of rage, Chad's dad yelled, "Your attitude stinks! You're grounded for a week. Now go to your room and don't come out until I tell you."

Chad stormed to his room, slammed the door, and turned on his radio as loud as it would go. Not to be outdone, his dad opened the door and angrily yelled, "Turn that thing down before I throw it out the window!" "Go ahead," Chad yelled. "See if I care!"

Jared is the father of four-year-old Rob. When Rob accidentally knocked over his milk at the breakfast table, Jared yelled, "What's the matter with you? Why can't you be more careful?"

Thirty-two-year-old June was trying to cope with a hectic job, two children, and a husband who wouldn't lift a finger to help around the home. After a long and hard day at work, her children got into a shoving and shouting match. June stormed into the children's bedroom, grabbed one under each arm, half threw them on the bed and angrily told them, "I'm sick and tired of your fighting." Then she gave them each several hard swats and told them to stay in their rooms until she said they could come out.

If these explosions sound familiar, you are not alone. All parents occasionally get angry with their children. However, for the sake of our children, we must be careful how we treat them when we're angry. We need to learn to handle our anger so that we don't frighten, depress, or alienate our children in the process. And we need to learn to resolve our anger, so that we can discipline in love instead of punish them in anger.

115

"But," you might reply, "if I don't lose my temper, my children will conclude I have gone soft and try to get by with murder." Not at all. Being loving doesn't mean being permissive. As a matter of fact, it is only after you mellow out your impulsive anger that you can discipline your children for their growth. Until then, you will be punishing them to vent your anger and get even.

A BIBLICAL PERSPECTIVE

The apostle Paul wrote: "Fathers, provoke not your children to anger, lest they be discouraged."[1] And Proverbs states, "A gentle answer turns away wrath, but a harsh word stirs up anger."[2] These verses tell why mishandled parental anger can be so devastating. It plants seeds of depression and anger in our children's hearts. And if we keep fertilizing those seeds with angry punishment, they may grow into lasting emotional wounds.

Think about how you would feel if someone two or three times your size lost his temper and hit or threatened you. No matter how justified his anger was, wouldn't you feel angry, frightened, or depressed? Parental anger is designed to intimidate our children into doing what we want or to make them suffer for disobeying our wishes. But few things chop at a child's feelings about himself more sharply than being angrily accused, threatened, or punished. Demeaning words like "clumsy," "lazy," or "irresponsible" are emotional hand-grenades, destroying a child's self-esteem. And it should go without saying that striking children in anger or giving them a verbal lashing is even more painful. That's why the Bible encourages us to control our anger. Proverbs says, "A fool gives full vent to his anger, but a wise man keeps himself under control."[3]

If you are frustrated and at wit's end, I'm not trying to make you feel guilty. I don't want you to repress your anger or think that you should make it vanish with a little willpower: anger doesn't work that way. Mishandled anger, however, can seriously damage children.

ISN'T ANY ANGER HELPFUL?

The Bible doesn't say that all anger is bad. Jesus got angry at the money changers in the temple because they had turned the Jewish house of worship into a commercial racket and were taking advantage of people. And he got angry at the Pharisees because they claimed he was casting out demons by the power of Beelzebub instead of God.[4] The apostle Paul tells us to be angry without sinning.[5] But, interestingly, the Bible doesn't record one instance of Jesus being angry with a child.

Helpful anger focuses on the negative results of sin. It flows from love and a desire for the other person's best. Look at this verse:

> Though he brings grief, he will show compassion, so great is
> his unfailing love. For he does not willingly bring affliction or
> grief to the children of men.[6]

At the very time God is angry at the sinner, he loves him. By contrast, when most of us get angry with our children, we don't feel loving. We want to inflict a little pain. We may feel loving later, but at the moment anger outweighs our care.

I'll be the first to admit that when I got angry with Richard and Debbie, it usually wasn't because I was angry at their sin and lovingly desired their best. It was because they disobeyed me and upset me, and I wanted to even the score! But the Bible reminds us, "Do not repay evil with evil or insult with insult."[7] Here are ways of determining whether your anger is helpful or hurtful.

- Helpful anger is directed toward evil, and especially toward people who are misleading others and denying their sin.
- Hurtful anger is directed at anyone who frustrates us, or gets in the way of what we want.
- Healthy anger coexists with love and concern for the other person.
- Destructive anger wants revenge and at least temporarily obscures our concern for the other.
- Godly anger is not expressed in impulsive, destructive ways, and we are able to move beyond it once the problem has been solved.
- Hurtful anger repeatedly returns or is harbored for a long time.

A NEW GOAL

Why not take a minute right now and ask yourself, "When I correct my children, do I discipline them lovingly for their growth or do I punish them in anger?" If you tend to punish in anger, why not set a new goal? Decide that you will correct them firmly, but in love instead of anger. Decide that instead of venting your frustrations to get even, you will discipline to help them grow. And decide that instead of rubbing their noses in past misdeeds, you will try to foster the attitudes and actions you want them to have in the future. This doesn't mean you will never punish in anger again, but if you shift your goal from retaliation to growth, you will be taking a step that will change your children's lives—and probably your own!

DON'T WAIT UNTIL YOU LOSE IT

One of the best ways to avoid losing your temper is to pay attention to your emotional thermometer. When your temperature is rising, don't let your children get by with one thing after another as you gradually become more frustrated. Losing your temper is only the blastoff after a long countdown to launch. We lose our tempers when we feel helpless, lose control, or allow our children to push us to our breaking point. If you discipline your children *before* things get out of hand, you will have fewer problems with your temper. The minute your children start pushing you near your breaking point, tell them your expectations and the discipline they will receive if they don't settle down. Then, if they disobey, implement the consequence. You won't be upset, because you haven't let things get out of control, and your children won't feel mistreated, because they knew what was coming.

BITE YOUR LIP

Once you have started to lose your temper, take the next step. *Restrain your first impulse.* The minute you feel your anger welling up inside, count to ten (or ten thousand!). Most of the hurt to children done by anger comes from failing to restrain our first impulse. Instead of lashing out with attacking comments like "You're so stupid" or "What's the matter with you," restrain yourself.

You may need to try a few self-disciplining tactics before you find out what works for you. Some parents can just count to ten and

© 1991 Bil Keane
Dist. by Cowles Synd., Inc.

"They look so sweet and peaceful when they're asleep. You wonder how they could ever yell at us during the day."

remind themselves that they are about to do something they will regret later. Others may need to leave the room or go outside for a while. Take a walk, call a friend, or go shopping. Let your spouse take charge of the children for a few hours. Whatever your method, find a way to restrain your first angry impulse.

TALK IT OVER

Once when my wife, Kathy, was furious with our son, she called her best friend Alice to tell her how she felt. When Alice asked Kathy, "Why is Richard making you so mad?" Kathy answered,

119

"He's acting just like his father!" Once Kathy understood this, she could start working on the real problem—me!

Letting off steam to a friend is a great way to handle angry feelings. It can also help you understand *why* you are so angry, so you can address the real problem.

TAKE A TIME OUT

If you are still too upset to discipline, let your mate handle the discipline or simply tell your children, "I'm too upset right now. After I settle down we'll have to talk this over." With that, you set an example of self-restraint for your children without ignoring the problem. This builds security and trust, because your children know you won't abuse them with your anger even though you must correct them.

LOOK FOR A PATTERN

If you are like most of us, one or more of your children has certain traits or habits that trigger your temper like someone tossing a lighted match into a pile of dry leaves. There are also certain days or times in a day when your temper is more likely to flare. For example, aren't you more likely to lose your temper with your children when you have already had a hard day? Do you get angry when you feel helpless? Do you lose it with your children when you are angry at your spouse? Do you lose your temper when you have to keep reminding your children to do their chores or pick up after themselves? Questions like this can help you understand and manage your anger.

If you haven't already noticed a pattern to your anger, start keeping track. When our children were young, I realized I got especially angry when they misbehaved in public. I was a psychologist, and they were making me look bad! As soon as I realized that I was getting mad because of my own ego instead of any serious misbehavior on my children's part, I decided to let Richard and Debbie be normal kids, even if they didn't always make me look good. From then on, I didn't get nearly so bent out of shape.

Once you have determined what triggers your temper, you can start working on your part of the problem. If you take your anger out on your children when you are really angry at your spouse, start working on the problem with your mate. If you are often upset during the evening, maybe you need to arrange some time for yourself late each afternoon or as soon as you return home from work. If mornings are the problem, work out a better schedule for your children with clear consequences for each task they fail to perform on time. And if you realize your children are pushing your emotional buttons (for example, they remind you of yourself or of a big brother or sister who used to bug you), start working on that. Sometimes it's hard to admit we take out our own frustrations on our children, but we do. By facing our own problems first, we can discipline our children for their own good.

DON'T SWEAT THE SMALL STUFF

Several years ago Harmon Killebrew, the second leading home run slugger in American League history, was inducted into the Baseball Hall of Fame. During the ceremony, Mr. Killebrew described his indebtedness to his parents. He recalled a day he and his brother were playing in the yard and his mother complained, "You're tearing up the grass." Killebrew's dad quickly spoke up and told his wife, "We're not raising grass, we're raising boys."

Harmon Killebrew's dad had the right perspective. Grass can be replaced, but the brief years of childhood can't. It's a big help to put your children's actions into life-long—even eternal—perspective. When your children break your favorite vase or stain the new carpet, ask yourself, *What is more important in the long run, a vase, the carpet, or my relationship with my children?*

As parents of grown children, my wife and I now wish we hadn't gotten so bent out of shape over the little things our children did. We realize that the good times with them and their feelings of safety and comfort with us were much more important than a few misbehaviors that seemed so exasperating at the time. Our experience reminds me of the plaque I saw on a business office wall. It read, "Rule One: Don't Sweat the Small Stuff. Rule Two: Everything Is Small Stuff." Of course, everything isn't "small stuff," but twenty years from now a lot of things that upset us about our children will seem that way.

ASK WHAT YOU CAN LEARN

Some parents have a favorite Bible verse. It's usually "Children, obey your parents."[8] I used to have a "most unfavorite verse." It was Romans 8:28. The King James Version reads, "And we know that all things work together for good to them that love God, to them who are the called according to *his* purpose." Only one verse in the Bible seemed worse. That was 1 Thessalonians 5:18, which says, "In everything give thanks: for this is the will of God in Christ Jesus concerning you." I had heard so many Christians describe how their lives were falling apart or how their children were on drugs or pregnant out of wedlock and then force a false smile as they said, "But we're praising God anyway" or, "All things work together for good." It seemed phony to me—like God wanted us to deny the reality of pain and sorrow in our lives. But then I studied these verses more carefully.

The New International Version (NIV), as well as other translations of the Bible, corrects the misimpression of the King James Version that "all things work for good." The fact is, some things don't work for good; some things are evil, and some things work for ill. The NIV translates Romans 8:28, "*In* all things God works for the good of those who love him, who have been called according to his purpose (italics mine)." First Thessalonians 5:18 is better translated, "*In* everything give thanks," not "*For* everything give thanks." It's not that all things work *for* good, but that even *in* bad things, God is working to bring something good. And we are not to give thanks *for* everything, but *in* everything.

In other words, even in difficult situations we can be growing and grateful that God is with us. These verses actually present a radically different approach to the frustrations of being a parent. We can get angry, blame our children, and be upset when they fall short of our expectations, or we can use the frustration and pain of parenthood to grow, to find what is important in life, to see areas where we need to change, and to become more loving, mature people.

Let me give you a practical example of how you can apply this principle. Let's say your son spills milk on your clean tablecloth. Your first impulse is to angrily leap to your feet and say, "What's the matter with you? I've told you to be careful." But wait a minute. How important is spilled milk in the light of eternity and your child's seventy-plus years on this planet? If you react angrily, you will make your child more fearful and probably depressed or angry. This certainly isn't your goal. What you want to do is help your son not spill milk again. You will do that better by reacting calmly rather than in anger.

So how could you react differently? How about using the unfortunate incident as an opportunity to become more patient and sensitive with your children? Simply say, "Whoops. Those things happen. Let's clean it up." Or you might even learn to defuse the situation with a little humor, as long as it isn't at your child's expense. You could say, "Uh-oh. It looks like some cow is going to have to work overtime!" Comments like this relax children and help them feel like you are on their side. They don't need to be told that spilling milk isn't good. They don't want to make a clumsy mistake any more than you want them to. At times like that, what they need is encouragement and support. When you are calm instead of angry, you help them do better next time.

A friend shared the following story with me. Thanksgiving dinner had just begun. The table was picture-perfect, from the china to the freshly pressed tablecloth. As things got underway, one of the children knocked over his milk. Talking halted and all eyes glared at the child as the puddle of milk soaked into the tablecloth. The silence was finally broken by Grandpa when he said, "I think this is too big a burden for one child to bear," and he reached out and pushed over his own glass! I'm not sure I want to recommend Grandpa's solution, but it shows sensitivity to how badly children can feel when they've done something wrong. And we might all be less uptight and more fun to be around if we were a little more like Grandpa.

Once you are committed to growing through your parental frustrations, an interesting thing happens. You will begin to see daily frustrations as opportunities to develop your character instead of chances to spew out your anger. Spilled milk doesn't have to be a disaster. It can be an opportunity to show patience and sensitivity and kindness to your children.

If you think the way you react to spilled milk is an insignificant problem, think again. Just this week in a university class, my students were discussing experiences that helped them feel good or bad about themselves while they were growing up. A twenty-year-old student's eyes became tearful as she shared how her parents had angrily shamed her for spilling things at the dinner table fifteen years earlier. The incident was burned into her memory.

"I" MESSAGES

I'm not encouraging you to deny your anger or fake that you aren't angry when you are. I'm simply suggesting that if you know what is upsetting you, and if you realize how insignificant some of your children's actions will seem to you in twenty years, you won't get so infuriated. And even when you are, you can manage your angry feelings in nondestructive ways. The best way to do that is to give your children an "I" message instead of a "you" message. Don't exclaim, "You make me so mad." That is an accusatory statement that blames your anger on your children. And actually, your children can't *make* you mad. They can't drill a hole in your skull, pour in some "mad" powder, and ignite it. They may do things to which you respond with anger, but they don't *force* you to be angry. You become angry based on your perception of the situation, your own tolerance level, and your own sensitivities.

When you need to tell your children you are angry, simply tell them "I am angry" or "When you do that, I get angry." "I" messages communicate crystal clearly without blaming or attacking. After all, how would you feel if a giant got angry at you and yelled, "You make me so mad"? I suspect you would feel a little intimidated and fearful! But if the giant says, "I'm angry," you can at least hope that he realizes you aren't totally to blame for his anger.

RECAP

Overcoming anger is a lot like learning patience. It takes time. If you have a problem with your temper, don't expect it to disappear overnight, and don't make a vow to never get angry again. It has taken you twenty-five or thirty years to get the way you are and if you are like most parents, you will change an inch at a time, not by leaps and bounds. If you try to repress your angry feelings, you will fail. Instead, decide that you are going to gradually move in the direction of being more kind and patient. Set a goal of disciplining instead of punishing and learn to discipline before things get out of hand. Commit yourself to restraining your first angry impulse. Take time from the heat of the moment to talk your frustrations over with a friend. Look for the hidden causes behind your anger. Learn to ignore the small stuff. And be willing to grow.

Notes

1. Colossians 3:21 (KJV).
2. Proverbs 15:1.
3. Proverbs 29:11.
4. Matthew 21:12–13, Matthew 12:22–27.
5. Ephesians 4:26.
6. Lamentations 3:32–33.
7. 1 Peter 3:9.
8. Ephesians 6:1.

CHAPTER 11

Building Your Child's Self-Image

When I was a doctoral candidate at the University of Kentucky, I held a part-time job administering intelligence tests to four-year-old children who were applying for admission to a private kindergarten. One Saturday morning a young mother brought her daughter to my office for testing.

"Hi, Ashley! How are you this morning?" I said cheerfully. Ashley grabbed her mother's skirt and started crying. "Have you seen the fish in our new aquarium?" I asked, trying to win her favor. "Waah," she cried again, as she held tightly to her mother. "Would you like to come into my office and play some games?" I asked, using all the psychology I could muster. But Ashley buried her head in her mother's dress and held on tight. She was scared stiff.

An hour and a half later, little Drew arrived. "Hi," I said. "How are you this morning?" "Fine," Drew enthusiastically replied. "How are you?" "Great," I answered. "Have you seen our fish?" "Yes, we have some guppies at home," Drew said alertly. "Let's play some games," I said. "Good!" Drew replied as he walked confidently into my office.

What a contrast! At four years of age, Drew was an alert, confident little guy. Ashley was insecure and heading for problems. I thought to myself, *What will these kids be like in a few years?* Unless things change, when speech class rolls around, Ashley will be tense, nervous, and upset. Drew will have no problem. If they join a church, Drew could be the chairman of a visitation committee. Ashley would be scared to death to knock on a door and meet a stranger.

127

The difference was their self-concept, their self-image, or their self-esteem. Though I'm sure he didn't stop to think about it, Drew liked himself. Since he felt confident and at ease with himself, he assumed strangers would like him too. He looked at me as a potential friend. Ashley, however, had a poor self-concept. Since she didn't feel very good about herself, she assumed no one else would either. That's why I was a potential threat.

FROM THE INSIDE OUT

Our self-concept is the mental picture or image we have of our bodies, our brains, and our personalities. Some of us have largely positive thoughts and feelings about ourselves. We know we make mistakes and have weaknesses, but we also know we have some God-given abilities and at least a reasonable share of positive attributes. This lets us feel good about ourselves. Others of us, like little Ashley, are riddled with negative thoughts and feelings. We constantly think we are deficient, inferior, or inadequate. We are afraid to meet new people, take risks, or make decisions because we don't have enough confidence in ourselves.

Your children's self-concept is one of the most vital keys to their fulfillment and success in life. Psychological research shows that children with positive self-concepts tend to achieve more at school and get along better with their peers. They like other children and are more cooperative and kind. They are also more resilient and aren't shattered when things don't go their way. Children with poor self-concepts are more likely to be depressed. They may be under-achievers and may have difficulty getting along with others. When they are young, they are more likely to misbehave to get attention or to withdraw and give up. Even if they are deeply loved by people around them, children with poor self-concepts have difficulty believing these expressions of love. Adolescents with poor self-concepts are more likely to get pregnant, fall into drug use or delinquency, feel depressed, and become suicidal.

Even our children's relationship with God is impacted by their self-concepts. Children with poor self-concepts have a hard time experiencing God's love. Since they think they are so unimportant, untalented, and worthless, they assume God must not love them or be interested in their lives.

Earlier, we looked at six ways to discipline your children. But disciplining is only one aspect of successful parenting. It is even more important to know how to nurture your children's inner lives—their thoughts and feelings about themselves. This will be the spring out of which their attitudes and behavior toward others will flow. Jesus said, "Out of the overflow of the heart the mouth speaks."[1] In other words, our words and actions come from our inner lives. If a person has a positive self-concept, that view will be reflected outward by liking and getting along with others, and being a happy, well-adjusted person.

This is illustrated well by the following story:

> An aged man sat at the entrance to a city. He was approached by a stranger who was looking for a new place to live. "What type of people live in this city?" the newcomer asked. "What type of people lived in the city you left?" the old man wanted to know. "Oh, they were wonderful people, very kind," replied the newcomer. "I hated to leave." "You will find the people here to be just as kind and wonderful as those you left behind," the old man said.
>
> A second traveler paused and asked the same question. Again, the old man wanted to know, "What kind of people lived in the city you left?" "Oh, they were terrible people, mean and selfish," he replied. "I suggest you look for another town," said the old gentlemen. "You will find the people of this city to be the same way."

Scott was the president of a large corporation. He was wealthy, active in his church, and had a fine family. From all outward appearances, he seemed to have it made. He should have felt great about himself. But his inner feelings were another story. He told me, "Bruce, I feel like a complete failure. Sometimes life doesn't seem worth living. I guess I know I'm successful, but I don't feel that way inside."

As we talked, it became obvious why Scott was never satisfied with himself. As a boy, he could never please his father. If he picked up the family room, his father complained that he hadn't straightened up the living room as well. If he got an A-, he should have gotten an A. When he fought for his toys with his brother, he was scolded for being selfish. And if he complained about anything, he was accused of being ungrateful. After being on the receiving end of constant criticism for eighteen years, Scott concluded that he could never do enough to satisfy his father. But he still didn't give up. He went off to college, where he graduated with honors. Then he started his own company and worked long hours until he became a millionaire. But even then Scott wasn't happy, because his life was dominated by his inner picture of himself as a boy who never did anything quite well enough.

Like Scott, your children's self-concepts will be born in childhood, and you will be the midwife. When you "ooh" and "aah" at the cute things they do as babies, you are telling them, "We like you. You are good." When you share your toddlers' excitement as they run across the living room, you are telling them, "That's great. I love to see you enjoying life and exploring your world." And when you listen attentively and share their excitement or their struggles at school, you are telling them, "You matter. You are a valuable, significant person, and I love you." Little by little, these affirming looks and words help children see themselves as lovable, gifted, important people.

But if our babies cry and we ignore them, we are subtly telling them, "Who cares? You don't matter." When we are too busy to take an interest in their days at school, we are telling them, "You aren't important." And if we criticize them or compare them unfavorably to others, we are telling them, "There is something fundamentally wrong with you." Our comments and our ways of relating to our children hold up mirrors that tell them how we think they should feel about themselves. For better or worse, children almost inevitably believe their parents' judgments.

As children spend more time outside the home, they encounter new "mirrors." Teachers, peers, pastors, and relatives add their evaluations to our children's attitudes toward themselves. Although these mirrors aren't as important as Mom's and Dad's, children still believe a great deal of what these other people see in them. If they are told, "You're fat and ugly," they will feel that way, even if they aren't. In fact, this is why awkward or overweight adolescents who grow into beautiful women often still feel unattractive. They believe the painful judgments of their high school peers, and they can't forget the mirror that used to be held up to them every morning.

THREE CORNERSTONES OF SELF-ESTEEM

Your children's self-image is built on three main attitudes or convictions. They need to feel at a deep emotional level:

- I am lovable.
- I have abilities and gifts.
- I am worthwhile.

Like the legs of a three-legged stool, each of these beliefs is equally important. Children who feel lovable have a good sense of *belonging*. They feel comfortable relating to other people. Children who believe they have a reasonable share of abilities feel *confident*. They are willing to tackle age-appropriate responsibilities, try new things, and compete with others at school and at play. Children who believe their thoughts and feelings matter when important decisions are made feel *worthwhile*. They expect to be respected and treated with dignity.

Notice that these three ingredients are the same ones we discussed in chapter 3 when we asked why children misbehave. Now we will see that those needs don't determine only your children's behavior, they also determine their self-image—the fundamental way they think and feel about themselves.

I Am Lovable

The first ingredient of a healthy self-image is the assurance that you are loved. Everyone needs to feel loved, and children are no exception. Their single greatest need is to know they belong to us, that they are so special and unique that we wouldn't trade them for anything in the world. Children who know they are loved have one of life's greatest gifts. Feeling loved enables them to love others, to feel good about themselves, and to make it through the tough and lonely times of life.

You may be thinking, "I love my children, so this won't be a problem." And perhaps it won't. But it is not enough to love our children. We must express our love in ways that our children understand, feel, and experience. It's not *being* loved that matters; it's *feeling* loved. We parents have to keep pouring out our love or it runs through our children's young minds like water through sand. Only as they receive daily, tangible expressions of our love will they develop a solid inner picture of themselves as lovable human beings.

If you have spent several days away from a fourteen- to twenty-four-month-old toddler, you may have seen his difficulty remembering your love. It's not unusual for a child this age to actually run the other direction when a parent returns—or at least keep a safe distance and eye the parent warily. That's because young toddlers haven't yet developed a solid inner picture of themselves in a loving relationship with their moms and dads. For a moment, they feel as though they are with strangers. It takes about three years for a newborn to develop that solid picture of himself as a loved, valued human being. This self-portrait may be severely corrupted if he isn't consistently shown and given love in the years that follow, but the initial picture is built up in the first three years of life.

Once these internal self-portraits develop, they last us a lifetime. For example, right now I can picture where my wife and children are and recall some very positive feelings about their love for me. Even if I don't consciously think about them, these deep feelings keep me company and allow me to feel loved throughout the day.

The *kind* of love children receive is as important as the amount. Children need to be loved the way God loves us, with no strings attached. Messages that tell children, "I love you if. . ." or "I love you when. . ." don't do the trick. Conditional love strikes fear in the hearts of children, and it shakes up their inner picture of themselves as lovable human beings. Children need to know we love them exactly the way they are, warts and all! When they experience unconditional love, they develop deep-seated feelings of being lovable people. Children who feel this way about themselves can bounce back and keep going when they lose a friend, fail to make the cheerleading squad, or face some other setback.

I saw this happen with our daughter, Debbie, when she was a high school sophomore. One morning before school, she was having a tough time getting her hair the way she wanted it. After struggling in front of the mirror for several minutes, Debbie finally announced, "Oh well, they will just have to take me like I am!" Unlike many adolescent girls, Debbie didn't throw a fit or break into tears because her "look" was off. She felt good enough about herself to know that people would accept her just the way she was. And if they didn't, that was their problem! That's the kind of resilience that comes from a positive self-concept.

Here are some things you can do to be sure your children feel deeply loved:

- Show love physically. Hugs and playful touches may say more than words.
- Make direct eye contact when you are talking. It tells children that you care.
- Be an active listener. When your children are talking, don't read the newspaper, watch TV, or give them half of your attention. Repeat back to them a summary of what they've shared with you to let them know you understand.
- Tell them you love them.
- Spend some mutually enjoyable time together every day. On busy days, ten to twenty minutes just before bedtime may be fine. On weekends and holidays, plan extended times. Have a family picnic. Camp out or go to your local library or amusement park. Make a date and take them out to lunch.
- Do special things to let your children know you are thinking of them. When my children were young, I brought them matchbooks and little bars of soap when I went on business trips around the country.
- Watch your children playing. You are never squandering time when you watch your children or play with them. Play is real life for children. Watching them tells them you are interested in them and their happiness.
- Watch your anger. Few things make children feel less loved than being verbally attacked by an angry parent.
- Never compare your children to each other or to other children.
- Watch your priorities. If you aren't careful, you might spend more time on tasks like cleaning, making a living, doing dishes, washing clothes, and yardwork than you do with your

children. Lower your material standard of living if you have to, to spend more time with your children. After all, they are incredibly more important.

- Don't let television rob your family of times together. TV can be great if you watch a good show and then discuss it, but don't let it become a substitute for family time together. Talk, play, and work together. Don't become a couch-potato parent.

- Above all, take an interest in your children. Take their opinions seriously. Let them know they matter. And let them know you love them and enjoy them. No one on their deathbed has ever said, "I wish I had spent more time at work and less time with my children!"

© 1991 Bil Keane
Dist. by Cowles Synd., Inc.

"You hafta listen to me with your eyes, Daddy. Not just your ears."

I Am Confident

Confidence is the second ingredient of a good self-concept. Confident children aren't afraid to meet new people. They are spontaneous and alert. They speak up in class, try new activities, are curious, and enjoy learning. They are neither extremely shy nor overbearing. Children who don't develop a healthy sense of confidence feel anxious or inferior. They either shy away from new challenges because they believe they will fail, or they overcompensate by becoming overbearing or controlling.

Children develop confidence when they have success in life and when others recognize and affirm their abilities. They lose confidence when they are criticized or overprotected, or when their thoughts, feelings, and contributions aren't taken seriously.

Brett Lee and his father were driving past a new car dealer when Brett spotted a bright red sports convertible. With excitement in his voice, he asked, "Dad, can we get a convertible next time?" "Of course not, Brett," Mr. Lee replied sternly. "Convertibles are dangerous, impractical, and expensive!" With that, the conversation ended and Brett sank quietly down into his seat.

Mr. Lee didn't know how to say no without making his son feel like he was asking a dumb question. Think how differently Brett would have felt if the conversation had gone like this:

Brett: Dad, can we get a convertible next time?

Mr. Lee: Would you like one?

Brett: I think it would be great! We could drive around town with the top down and wave at our friends.

Mr. Lee: That does sound like fun. What else do you like about convertibles?

Brett: Oh, that's about all, I guess.

Mr. Lee: Yes, that would be fun. But there are some problems, too. A convertible costs more than a regular car, plus it doesn't hold the warm air as well in the winter. Some people say they're not too safe. How do you think they would hold up in a crash?

Brett: I don't know, but I guess if it rolled over, everyone would get smashed.

Mr. Lee: Yeah, I'm afraid you're right. But it would sure be fun to drive!

Brett: Yes, as long as you didn't get in a wreck.

Notice the difference? In the second scenario, Brett emerges feeling better about himself because his dad respected his opinions and took him seriously. His dad confirmed Brett's opinion that convertibles *are* fun. Brett also learned to look at the pros and cons in making a decision, because his dad asked him a question that made him think. Instead of putting Brett down, he helped him come to a better decision for himself. That built up Brett's confidence.

No parent wakes up in the morning thinking, *I wonder what I can do to undermine my child's self-confidence today*. But sometimes we undermine their confidence almost as if we had. We criticize our children, focus on their failures, tell them how they can do better, and compare them to their brothers and sisters. Meaning to be helpful, we tell our son, "The dance routine was good, Andy, but you could have done a little better." And what sticks in Andy's mind? Andy thinks, *I should do better. I'm not doing well enough*. Another day we tell him, "Your brother doesn't leave his chores half done. Why do you?" Our criticisms and comparisons are like a small toxic leak, and Andy develops more and more self-doubt. If we aren't careful, we will poison his self-confidence and Andy will come to believe he can't do anything right.

Our motives for focusing on our children's failures may be admirable. We want to rear well-behaved, successful children. So we think, *If I make him realize he isn't doing well, he will improve*. And some children do. But if we don't balance each word of criticism with pages of praise and affirmation, we may sacrifice the long-range goal of a good self-image for the present satisfaction of a high-quality performance. Children may need an occasional word of constructive criticism, but be very careful to place your emphasis on what they are doing well. Many early achievers burn out or drop out later because they have been living too long with excessive parental pressure. It is more important for children to develop confident, wholesome attitudes toward themselves and you, than for them to be exceptional performers. Children who feel confident will eventually perform well even if they don't do everything the way you want while they are growing up. Here are some ways to build your children's confidence:

- Be an encourager. We should be our children's biggest fans.
- Praise and compliment them freely. Don't offer effusive praise for a half-hearted job, but do give frequent, loving affirmations of both your children's efforts and their accomplishments.
- Avoid overprotection. If you worry too much and overprotect your children, you will pass your fearfulness on to them.
- Keep criticism to a minimum. I often tell parents, "It takes ninety-nine compliments to make up for one criticism." Children remember our negative comments, but easily forget the positive ones. Emphasize the good they're doing.
- Encourage exploration. Children develop confidence when they are able to try new things, even when there is a little risk involved.
- Assign chores and teach skills that are useful around the home. As children grow up, they should learn how to prepare a hot breakfast, use basic tools, and put gas in the car. Chores tell children they are needed and help develop their abilities and gifts, furthering their confidence.
- Work with your children on more complex tasks around the home, but don't do their work *for* them. That robs them of a chance to develop confidence in their own abilities.
- Don't be a perfectionist. If your expectations are too high, your children will feel like failures. Reward good efforts, sincere desires, and jobs that aren't done perfectly the first time. Let them know we all fail.

- Get your children involved in activities outside the home where they can experience success. School band, choir, athletics, clubs, and part-time jobs all help build children's confidence.
- Encourage age-appropriate independence. Give them an allowance and gradually increase it, along with their responsibility for purchasing their own clothing and other needs. Children must steadily become more independent if they are going to have strong self-images. Don't push your children out too soon, but don't hang on too long. Gradually cut the apron strings and help them become more independent.

I Am Worthwhile

A story is told about a family that went out to dinner at a local restaurant. When the waitress asked Taylor, the young boy of the family, "What would you like to eat?" he confidently announced, "I'll have a hamburger." Taylor's mother interrupted and authoritatively told the waitress, "He'll have roast beef!" "And what would you like on your hamburger?" the waitress asked. "I'll have mustard and ketchup," he replied. With a stern look, Taylor's mother said, "He'll have some green beans!" Ignoring the mother, the waitress continued, "And what would you like to drink?" The boy answered, "I'll have a Coke!" With her stern motherly look, Taylor's mom firmly said, "He'll have milk!" The waitress left and soon returned with exactly what Taylor ordered. With a sense of amazement, he turned to his mother and said, "Gee, Mom. She thinks I'm real!"

Are you ever like this mother? Do you ever essentially tell your children, "Your opinion doesn't matter. You are just a child"? Or do you make other comments that imply, "You children are fine and we love you. But when you get big, you'll be more important"? If you do, be careful. Remember that your words are mirrors to your children. When you take your children's opinions seriously, they walk away with a sense of value, dignity, and respect. When you don't, they feel insignificant, unimportant, a nuisance, and a bother.

Several years ago I read a great little article on how parents speak to their children. I can't remember where I read it, but it went something like this:

> Can you imagine what it would be like if we spoke to our friends the way we speak to our children? Clint and Bev, a married couple, come to our home for dinner and we greet them at the door. "What's the matter?" we ask disapprovingly. "You're fifteen minutes late." Then we tell Clint, "Shut the door. Were you born in a barn?" When Clint sits comfortably on the couch we tell him, "Don't slouch. Don't you know that's bad for your back?" And at the dinner table we tell him, "Get your elbows off the table, Clint. Don't you have any manners?" Then we tell him, "Finish your vegetables or you can't have any dessert." Then we threaten to send him away from the table. Each of our comments say, "Clint, what's wrong with you?" or "Why can't you be better than you are?"

Of course, we would lose all our friends if we talked like that. But we talk to our children that way and don't give it a second thought. No wonder they don't feel special!

Another way to undercut your children's sense of worth is by giving them a curt, "Because I said so!" when they ask you, "Why?" This simple comment, though well-intended, actually tells children, "You aren't important enough to get an answer." Of course you can't have a thirty-minute discussion every time your children ask you "why." Four-year-olds can go on asking "why" for hours. But if you want your children to believe their thoughts are important, you need to give them respectful answers to appropriate questions. It lets them know you take them seriously.

When children are eager to tell you a story, by all means, let them. If you have ever rushed home with some great news only to have your mate say, "Later. I'm busy," you know what I mean. Remember that feeling? You probably thought, *Oh well, I guess it wasn't that important!* followed by a tinge of hurt, anger, or rejection. The one who loved you most wouldn't take time to listen. When children want to talk, they need a listener. They don't need to hear, "Because I said so" or "Later, dear. Mommy's busy right now."

This doesn't mean you should drop everything you're doing and come running every time your child opens his mouth. But ask yourself, "What is my priority? Is what I'm busy with as important as my relationship with my son?" Dishes and lawns can wait. Children can't.

Remember the story of Jesus and the little children? Jesus was conducting some important business in Judaea. Hundreds had followed him, and he was healing people right and left. Just as he was having a vital discussion with the Pharisees, some children came to visit. Jesus' disciples brushed them off and told them, "Can't you see he's busy? He has important things to do." But Jesus rebuked his mistaken disciples and told them, "Let the little children come to me, and do not hinder them, for the kingdom of heaven belongs to such as these."[2] Jesus took children seriously—he didn't tell them to wait! If you are too busy to listen to your children, you are too busy.

One day, as I was writing the first edition of this book, my son kept interrupting. He would say, "Daddy?" But when I looked up, he had nothing to say. After three or four times of the same thing, I realized he was really saying, "Daddy, will you play with me?" or "Daddy, do I matter?" I dropped my pen and went to the yard to play. Then we took a ride downtown. Soon Richard's somber mood turned to joy. He began to sing as we rode along. He knew he was more important than this book.

Here are ways you can let your children know they matter:

- Pay attention to your children's thoughts, feelings, and ideas. Draw them out and let them know you take their ideas seriously.
- Bring your children into as many family decisions as you can. Ask for their thoughts about what to have for dinner, what church to attend, and what car to buy. This tells children you think they have good ideas and that they are important to you.
- Give reasons for your rules. Try not to tell your children, "Because I said so." You don't have to defend every rule you have or give a lengthy answer, but telling children why they can't do something—or why they must—tells them you respect them.

- Never engage in character assassination. Labels like "clumsy," "slow," "stupid," "bother," "nuisance," and "pest" undermine your children's sense of dignity and value.
- Don't punish in anger. Angry punishment undercuts a growing child's self-respect. Gentle discipline helps children feel loved and valuable.
- Set realistic expectations. Try not to raise a perfectionist or a workaholic. When children think we only approve of them when they are succeeding or doing their best, their feelings of self-worth become tied too closely to their performance. Children need to be able to fail, to be average, and still feel good about themselves. They shouldn't always have to try to be the best or feel guilty if they are taking life a little easy.
- Avoid shame and guilt motivation. Shame and guilt undermine a child's sense of worth and value. Use positive motivations instead.

BUT WHAT ABOUT HUMILITY?

Some Christian parents are afraid to build up their children's self-esteem because they are afraid they will become sinfully proud. But pride is different from a positive self-concept. Proud people think they are better than others, while people with positive self-concepts value other people as equals. Prideful people are selfish, but people with good self-concepts like to share. And proud people deny their problems and limitations, whereas people with good self-concepts can admit their faults and failures.

The Bible has a lot to say about the attitude we should have toward ourselves and others, including children. From the first chapter of Genesis to the last chapter of Revelation, the Bible stresses the high value God places on human beings. It tells us we were created in God's image.[3] It tells us we are the apex of his earthly creation.[4] It tells us that we are so important that Christ died for us.[5] It tells us God gifted each of us.[6] It tells us he loves us.[7] And it tells us we will spend eternity with him.[8]

It is a shame that some Christian parents who believe God created us and loves us, treat their children like they are worthless.

Apparently, they think the fact that we are sinners means that we are no good—but it doesn't. Christ valued us so highly that he was willing to die for us. If we follow Jesus' example, we will ascribe high significance and value to all children.

RECAP

Your children's self-esteem is one of their most prized possessions, but it is also one of the most fragile. Young children need years of love, encouragement, and support in order to develop confidence in themselves and to feel loved and important. As their parent, you are the first and most important mirror from which they learn about themselves. If you repeatedly let them know you love them and appreciate their ideas and abilities, they will learn to feel good about themselves and be equipped to handle what life throws at them.

Notes

1. Matthew 12:34.
2. Matthew 19:14–15.
3. Genesis 1:26–27.
4. Psalms 8:5.
5. 1 Peter 1:18–19.
6. Romans 12:6–8.
7. John 3:16.
8. John 14:1–3.

CHAPTER 12

How *Not* to Talk with Your Children About Sex

While I was working on this manuscript, a mother phoned me from the Midwest. "Dr. Narramore," she said, "A few days ago my six-year-old daughter came home from visiting at her girlfriend's and asked me all kinds of questions about sex. I don't think I'm prudish," she went on, "but the questions made me uncomfortable."

Like this mom, many parents stiffen with fear the first time our children ask us about sex, or we find them playing "doctor" with a friend. We don't know what to do when we find a *Playboy* magazine under our son's mattress, when our teenage daughter reads nothing but Harlequin Romance books, or when our adolescent asks how far we think they should go on a date.

While a little anxiety is normal, sex education doesn't have to be a difficult or embarrassing chore. A little forethought and preparation can help you handle most aspects of your children's sexual education naturally in the course of everyday conversations. With a little planning, you will never have to say, "You will understand when you are older" or "Ask your daddy when he comes home."

MOMMY'S BOY, DADDY'S GIRL

Do you remember sitting on your bed at age twelve, listening to your mother or father struggling to tell you about the birds and the bees? Many adults think that's what sex education is all about. But that's only one small part of it. Much more important to your children's later sex life is their ability to treat others with respect, to love and be loved by other people. That is the foundation of good adult sexual attitudes and actions.

Children learn to love and be emotionally intimate in their relationships with their moms and dads. If they learn to be warm and loving with you, they will be able to love others the same way, and their sexuality will flow naturally out of their ability to be intimate with other human beings. If they don't feel close and comfortable with you, they are likely to have difficulties with intimacy and sexuality in later life. To put it succinctly: *The single most important determiner of your children's sexual adjustment will be their relationship with their most important sexual role models—you and your spouse.*

If a boy is going to grow up with healthy attitudes about his sexuality, he needs a good relationship with his father and mother. One cause of rampant homosexuality and sex role confusion is that many fathers are investing too little time and energy in their relationships with their children. Every boy needs a dad who asks him how his day went, draws him out, and listens between the lines. He needs a father who encourages and coaches him on new tasks, plays catch with him in the park, and provides a good example of what a boy can grow up to be. He needs a man he can respect and pattern his life after, a good role model.

A boy also needs a mother who is happy with herself and her role in life. He needs a mom who supports and affirms his masculine endeavors. And when he reaches dating age, he needs a mom who affirms his sexuality by telling him that any girl in school would be lucky to go out with him. When either parent is absent or unhappy in their own male or female role in life, it is tough for a boy to feel comfortable with his developing masculinity. For example, the combination of a domineering or over-indulgent mother and a passive, weak, or absent father is one cause of male homosexuality. The father's weakness leaves the male child without a model of masculinity, while the mother's over-involvement in the boy's life prevents him from separating from her emotionally and establishing his male identity. He becomes like his mother because he doesn't want to, or doesn't know how to, be like his father. Given this dynamic, his later homosexuality is related to a belated search for a relationship with a father substitute.

The same is true for a girl's sexual adjustment. If a mother has strong resentment toward men, she will undoubtedly pass that on to her daughter. Consequently, the girl will grow up believing men are weak, irresponsible, disinterested, cruel, or whatever else the mother believed. When a girl raised in this type of emotional atmosphere marries, she will tend to project those attitudes onto her husband, even if he is responsible, loving, and kind. And like boys looking for fathers, girls who can't connect with their mother may search for a substitute female connection through lesbianism.

Any conflicts parents have are also easily carried into their children's own marriages. Parents who fight continually, or who don't respect each other, are models of hostility rather than harmony between the sexes. This makes it difficult for the children to establish close loving connections with their spouse.

That's why biological information about sex is one of the least important parts of sexual education. The main ingredients of sexual adjustment are our attitudes toward ourselves, our parents, and members of the opposite sex. When a woman mistrusts men, or when a man believes women are tools to be used sexually, no amount of knowledge about the physiology of sex will help. But when two people grow into adulthood with good attitudes toward themselves and an ability to love others, they shouldn't have too much difficulty mastering the physical side of sexuality. Since most of this book is devoted to helping you improve the quality of your emotional relationships with your children, however, here are some specific suggestions on how to help your children develop healthy sex attitudes and values.

NATURALNESS IS THE KEY

When talking to your children about sex, your tone of voice and your attitude toward sex and the human body are more important than what you say. Naturalness is the key. If you feel comfortable with your body and enjoy your sexuality without shame or guilt, your children will be on their way to positive sexual adjustment. They will sense the positive attitude that smiles from behind your words. But if you are awkward or anxious, your children will sense your anxiety and learn to view sex as something hidden, mysterious, or bad.

Isn't it interesting that we approve of our children's curiosity in almost every area except sex and sexual organs? When a child asks, "What's this?" and points to a flower pot, we calmly tell him, "It's a flower pot." If he feels his ear, we think nothing of it. But let him feel his penis, and we freak out! No wonder children feel anxious and guilty over sex. We train them to be that way when we inject them with our own anxiety.

© 1991 Bil Keane
Dist. by Cowles Synd., Inc.

"I got an F in Sex!"

Sexual curiosity is as normal as any other curiosity, and as soon as our children have sufficient knowledge to satisfy their curiosity, they will move on to another topic. If you have children of both sexes, you are especially lucky. Your daughters will have opportunity to find out what a boy's penis looks like in the daily course of events. And your son will find out about the female anatomy just as naturally. There is absolutely nothing wrong with young children (preschool age) bathing together if they wish. This is a good way to let them satisfy their curiosity and learn something about their bodies.

If you only have one child, or if all of your children are the same sex, you can take advantage of visits by friends who have babies or young children. Your children can very naturally observe a baby being diapered or bathed. They may also occasionally see you and your spouse nude. This will give them chances to ask questions and to observe the basic anatomical differences between the sexes.

Of course, it's difficult to be natural and anxiety-free when talking about sex if you were reared in a home where sex was a taboo subject. One woman told me, "I'll never forget my first period. I had never heard a word about menstruation, and I panicked and ran to my mother. 'What's wrong?' I said, 'I'm bleeding!' My mother mumbled something about my period starting, gave me one of her tampons, told me I would be okay, and said she would get a book for me tomorrow. When I got married I vowed I would never let the same thing happen with my daughter. But she is ten now, and I'm afraid to talk to her!"

You may want to talk through your own anxieties with your spouse or a close friend or read some books on human sexuality. Attend a class or seminar on sexuality. If you have serious and deeply rooted anxieties, professional counseling may be in order. But one way or another, you need to become comfortable with your own sexuality. It's the only way you will be able to communicate healthier attitudes to your children.

YOU CAN'T BEGIN TOO EARLY

Nearly every time I speak to a group of parents, someone asks, "When should we begin our children's sexual education?" But just the way the question is phrased reflects a misconception. Sex education begins, whether we like it or not, when we hold our newborn in our arms for the first time. Sex education is tied up with our children's deepest feelings about themselves and their bodies. It includes an understanding of bodily parts and functions. And it includes their attitudes toward themselves, their parents, their friends, and their siblings.

If you try to relegate sex education to specific age, crisis points, books, or lectures you will miss the crucial point: sex education is a way of life. While you would not attempt to explain the menstruation cycle to a two-year-old, you should be prepared to frankly discuss the penis, the vagina, the breasts, and their respective functions as soon as your children begin to ask or show an interest. The three-year-old who asks, "Where do babies come from?" doesn't want a detailed explanation about conception, gestation, and intrauterine life. She just wants to know "where babies come from." "Mommy's tummy" is all she needs to know. Don't worry about your simplified explanation. She will return later to ask, "But how do they get into her tummy?" or "How do they get out?" As she grows older, her inquiries will call for increasing detail and accuracy. This is exactly as it should be. As children mature they can absorb the new information.

HANDLING QUESTIONS

Every child is full of questions. They will want to know how that woman over there got purple hair, why Daddy has to mow the lawn, why girls don't have penises, and how come only mommies have breasts. Try to answer the last two questions the same way you answered the first two: without showing embarrassment or surprise.

In our society, children come into contact with all kinds of sexual misinformation. If they know you are comfortable talking with them about sex, they will feel free to share their "findings" with you rather than keeping them secret and feeling confused, frightened, or guilty. If they know that you want them to ask questions and that talking about sex is entirely normal and routine, your children will begin to overcome their anxiety and secretiveness. Perhaps the single most damaging thing to good sexual adjustment is a feeling that sex is somehow secretive, dirty, or embarrassing. And since many of your children's friends will have that attitude, you need to let your children know that you are different, that you can handle their questions without embarrassment.

A second thing to keep in mind in handling children's questions is to *be direct*. Answer questions calmly and immediately. Evading the question or beating around the bush never helps a child's attitude toward sex. Direct, forthright answers help children feel comfortable with their bodies and their sexuality. An honest question deserves an honest answer.

When Richard was about five or six, we were driving along in the family car and out of the blue he turned to me and asked, "Daddy, what's ____?" "That's a word some people use for intercourse," I said. "You know what intercourse is?" "Yes," Richard said, and explained quite explicitly for his age. "Right," I said as we drove on. A moment later, Richard asked, "Dad, what's ____?" I replied, "That's just another way of saying bowel movement." No consternation, but direct explanation.

Soon Richard had another question—and then another. He went through a list of eight or ten slang words he had picked up from his first-grade friends. Each time I gave him a straight answer. After he exhausted all his questions, I asked him where he had learned those words. "From Jimmie," he replied. Then I said, "Richard, some children think their bodies are kind of funny, and they don't understand how they work. Maybe their parents are embarrassed to talk about their bodies, so they use words like ____, and ____. In our family, we think it's better to just say 'intercourse' or 'bowel movement.' God made our bodies so that we can eat food, digest it, and pass out the part we don't need. He also made us so we can enjoy our bodies and have children and start families. While there is nothing wrong with words like ____, ____, and ____, we think it's better to use the real words."

I am sure this forthright handling of potentially embarrassing questions went a long way in helping Richard avoid both "gutter language" and the sense of shame or dirtiness that may accompany it. Since that time, he has also felt free to come to me with other questions about his body and sex.

Here's a final guide to handling questions: don't give your children more or less than they are asking. Just like we can avoid giving children a frank answer, we can also overdo it. Don't be like the mother whose seven-year-old daughter came home from school and asked, "What's sex?" The mother could feel beads of sweat forming on her forehead. She sat her daughter down, took a deep breath, and plunged in. After mumbling and stumbling for several minutes, the daughter finally interrupted and said, "Mom, on a form I got at school today it said 'SEX, M or F.' What does that mean?"

WHEN CHILDREN DON'T ASK QUESTIONS

Since many of us have our own anxieties about sex, we are just as happy if our children don't bother to ask us any questions. In fact, we may feel relieved. But watch out. If your children are nearing school age and haven't raised a few questions about their bodies, where babies come from, and how boys and girls are different, it is probably time you look for ways to stimulate their curiosity or to let them know that these are good areas for discussion. You may begin by asking yourself if you have shied away from ever mentioning the penis, the vagina, the breasts, or other "sensitive" parts of your anatomy. If you have hesitated to talk frankly about the parts of your body or your children's, you can expect them to be just as reluctant. You need to get over your own anxiety in a hurry so you can talk about the body as naturally as you hope your child eventually will.

If you have a friend or a relative who is pregnant or has a new baby, you have an opportunity to ask your child if he knows how babies get their start in life. You may also pick up a little book that explains in simple language the process of reproduction. Don't just hand it to your children and say, "Call me if you have any questions." Sit down and read it with them, talking about it as you go. At Christmas you have an excellent opportunity if you read the story of Christ's birth to your children. Ask them if they know what it means to be a virgin. Explain the miracle of Christ's conception. There are scores of ways to naturally lead your children into a brief discussion. Don't be dramatic about it and don't give unnecessarily long or detailed explanations. But if you sense your children are a little hesitant to discuss their bodies, or that they may not be getting accurate information on sex, find ways to bring up the topic and encourage their questions and discussion.

NUDITY IN THE HOME

A young man in his twenties told me how in his childhood years, his mother continually paraded around their home in the nude. She believed that she was "free" and "liberated." Unfortunately, the son had a different interpretation. He believed his mother was exhibiting herself and trying to gain his attention. Years of this had stirred up serious sexual conflicts in this man. He was alternately embarrassed, stimulated, frightened, and ashamed of his mother's nudity. Needless to say, the effect on him wasn't healthy.

Some parents go to the opposite extreme. They *never* allow their children—especially children of the opposite sex—to see them naked. When a child walks in unexpectedly, these parents quickly grab a robe, run into the bathroom, or yell at their children not to look. This is almost as unhealthy as parading around the house naked.

A healthy approach is somewhere in the middle. Young children will occasionally walk into your bedroom when you are undressing or getting out of the shower. When that happens, calmly go about your business and put on your clothes as usual. Don't stand there naked and engage in a lengthy conversation, but don't dive under the bed either. If your seven-year-old child of the opposite sex comes in while you are taking a bath, go on with your business, chat a bit, and soon they will be on their way.

The same is true about your children's nudity. If your son decides to streak around the house naked, don't shame him or anxiously tell him, "Go get on some clothes!" And if your five-year-old daughter is acting like a cheerleader in the buff, she is really saying, "How do you like my body?" or "Can I be spontaneous and free?" You need to accept her developing awareness of her body's attractiveness by saying something like, "Hey, you are really a great cheerleader." Then give her a hug or playfully pat her bottom and say, "Don't you think it is about time the cheerleader gets dressed now?" That lets her know her body is fine and normal and she needn't be embarrassed about it. At the same time, it lets her know we generally wear clothes!

By pre-adolescence (around ten years of age), it's time to draw some clear boundaries about privacy. Simply tell your child, "At your age you need to have your privacy. Mom and Dad won't come into your room without knocking and you don't come into ours." That simple message tells your son or daughter, "You are growing up, and we will respect your increasing maturity."

WHEN CHILDREN EXPLORE

All children explore their bodies, and most children do some of their exploring with friends or siblings. This is normal, since anything that is unknown, hidden, or forbidden stimulates curiosity. One of the common ways children satisfy their curiosity about the body is to "play doctor." And what better game could they select, since doctors spend all day examining the human body? Toddlers and young preschoolers listen for heartbeats with their "stethoscopes" and prescribe everything from pills to an injection for their patient's ailments. As children approach kindergarten age it's not unusual to hear giggles coming from their room or to walk in to find your son or daughter stark naked with a friend examining each other's bodies.

Although that can be scary for a parent, try to stay cool. Remember, this is an entirely normal process. If your children were examining each other's foot or finger or nose you would think it was cute. It's only because they are examining their penis, vagina, or anus that you are frightened. It also helps to remember that you probably did a little sexual exploring yourself, and it didn't ruin you. In fact, it may have even satisfied your curiosity, and I'm sure you grew out of it naturally.

A good way to handle these unexpected situations is to say something like, "Hi, Doctor. How is your patient doing?" or "Doctor, my arm is hurting. Could you check it out?" That will bring a stop to their play rather quickly without creating any shame or guilt. Remember, it's God that made the human body. Later, you can tell your son or daughter, "Our bodies are really interesting, aren't they? It's amazing how God made us. What did you learn about our bodies playing doctor today?" This tells your children that their curiosity is good. It also gives you an opportunity to talk to them about their bodies. You can even take that opportunity to buy them a little book or pamphlet with pictures that you can read together. Instead of being afraid that your child is becoming a pervert, try to see their sexual exploration as a normal desire to know more about their bodies. It is an excellent opportunity for you to help them learn.

TIME IS ON YOUR SIDE

Like every part of your children's life, sexual growth and education is a process. Just because you've made a few mistakes or had some embarrassing moments doesn't mean that you have messed up your children's sexuality. As long as your children know that you like your body and theirs, they will gradually come to feel okay about theirs. And remember, you have the better part of two decades to communicate a positive attitude about sex. Even if you have lost several years, you will have a lot more chances. If you have been afraid to talk openly with your children, start talking with someone yourself—your spouse, a friend—or, if you feel very anxious or upset, a professional therapist. If you take a little time to work out your own anxieties and learn to communicate more openly and less anxiously with your children, you will find that you can have some very important and meaningful conversations with them about sex in the years to come.

RECAP

Sexual education is more than information. If you and your spouse have loving, kind relationships with your children, they will develop good feelings about themselves and others. This is the foundation for good sexual adjustment. You can build on this foundation by being natural about the human body and by providing information and giving direct, honest answers to your children's questions about sex and the human body.

CHAPTER 13

Working Mothers: Women in Two Worlds

The past twenty years have seen a dramatic rise in the number of mothers working outside the home. In the United States, one half of mothers with children under six years of age are employed. Some of those work by choice, but most work out of necessity. They either cannot live on their husbands' salary or they are the sole breadwinner.

During the 1960s and 70s, feminist leaders created new hopes of women finding fulfillment in the workplace. They suggested, at least by implication, that being "just a mother" was a boring job with few personal rewards. To be a whole person, women needed to find fulfillment in a career.

Two decades after the height of that movement, the struggle has shifted. Few in America would deny that women deserve equality with men in the workplace, but now that we have a consensus on that issue, women who are mothers still face tough decisions. It is one thing to have the social freedom, the opportunity, and the encouragement to work. It is another thing to be forced to work in order to feed yourself and your children. And it's still another thing to decide what is best for you, your children, and your family if you have a choice.

The toughest decision in the lives of many women today is how to balance work outside the home with the duties of family and child-rearing. In this chapter, we will look at two questions about working while you are rearing children. First, "If I have a choice, what should I consider before taking on a job?" Second, "If I do work, how can I handle the pressures my family and I are bound to face?"

TO WORK OR NOT TO WORK:
WHAT TO CONSIDER BEFORE YOU TAKE A JOB

If you are a mother hearing the call of the office, or if you are considering giving up your job to be a full-time parent, you have my sympathy. There are no easy answers. No one in this world is in precisely your situation, with your interests and abilities, your children, your husband or solo marital status, and your finances.

If you are like most mothers, you would stay at home if you could, at least while your children are young. A recent poll of one thousand households in southern California, for example, found that eighty percent of working mothers would quit their jobs to rear their children if they could manage it financially. That's a huge "if," of course. If you are a single parent, or you are living in an area with expensive housing, you may not have a choice. As Julie, the mother of three children, told me, "From the time our first child was a year old, I did a little day care. It was fun, and it gave Todd a playmate and me a little extra money. But when the twins came, it suddenly became more than a nice extra. If the five of us were going to get out of that apartment and into a house, I had to work. So I started a full-time day care business in my home."

Most working mothers are in a similar dilemma. Their families can't live on one income, they are the sole provider, or they have unexpected bills, so they have to work. Other mothers are more fortunate. They at least have a choice. But given the outrageous price of homes in some large cities, the only way they can afford a home or maintain a certain standard of living is to be a two-income family.

I have mixed feelings about mothers working when they don't have to. I like a nice house and a new car as much as the next person. But if a woman doesn't want to work, yet feels it is necessary to support the family's style of living, I wonder if it isn't time for her to sit down with her husband and evaluate their lifestyle. Is the physical and emotional fatigue, the pressures on the children and the husband, really worth the additional income? How much additional money will a second income actually bring in after paying taxes, hiring a babysitter or paying day care, and buying appropriate work clothes? And don't forget the extra travel expenses, lunches at work, union dues, and on and on. Sometimes, when you actually figure up the costs, you are sacrificing a huge amount of time and energy for a very small return.[1]

It takes courage, but I believe that many families should consider lowering their standard of living in order to get by on their current income. Some families may decide to move to a less expensive home or area of the country. Others place radical restrictions on their spending patterns. These are difficult measures, but the potential payoff in the quality of life for you and your children is tremendous. Jackie, a single mother, wrote me this moving letter:

> There is no job or no amount of money that could make me put Calvin in day care. He is going to be seven years old in three days. He's more than a third of the way to eighteen and out the door. I choose to have time with Calvin instead of money. Last year I lived on $7,000. I moved into the third-floor attic of some friends in a less-than-glamorous neighborhood. My car is eleven years old, but it's paid for and cheap to insure. All of our clothes come from yard sales. I found a part-time work study job at the university so I can attend graduate school and work at home on a computer. When Calvin started kindergarten, I found another job that allowed me to work from 8:30 to 1:00 P.M. each day. Now that he is in school full days I work until 3:00. But, before you feel sorry for me, I choose to do this. I choose to spend the time I could be working with my son and taking a few graduate courses to prepare myself for a career. I hope to have a productive career some day, but I will never have a more important ministry than my son. God has entrusted him to me, and I refuse to get distracted by accruing things. If the Lord hadn't worked out the jobs for me that he did, I would have seriously considered being a live-in nanny so I could be with Calvin.
>
> Getting by on this little also has its advantages. When I worry about being off work, I only have to worry about a few hundred, not thousands, of dollars. In addition to lots of time with my son, I have time to cultivate interests and hobbies. I have taken free or inexpensive courses in ballroom dancing, cake decorating, tax preparation, plumbing, and photography. I also have time for friends and to cultivate potential friendships.

I am not recommending Jackie's choice for everyone, but I think it deserves careful attention. It is easy to assume that you must maintain or improve your current standard of living, even if it means that you have to take a full-time job when, in actuality, you have a choice. I encourage you to look at some long-range goals and eternal perspectives. When your children are young, they need more time with you. As they get older, they can get by with less. When they go to kindergarten, you can work half-days without being away from them while they are home. When they go to first grade, you can work three-quarter time, and when they are in high school and have their own part time jobs or are involved in their own activities, you can work full-time.

Contrary to what we are led to believe, we don't have to have everything *now.* It would be great to take a job and have a nice house right away, but someday when your child is leaving home and you have the house all to yourself, you might think it's not that big of a deal.

There are some other things to consider before you enter the workplace as a mother. First, *all children need substantial amounts of time with their parents.* Regardless of age, sex, or personality, your children need for you or your spouse to be available. Ideally, preschoolers need a parent who spends a good bit of time with them throughout the day. School-aged children need parents who greet them in the morning, spend a little time together over breakfast, get them off to school, and greet them when they return. They also need parents who are good listeners and who spend quality time with them in the evening and on weekends. Children who have available parents feel emotionally anchored, secure, and loved. Children who don't, feel less secure and more anxious.

Notice that I said that children need available *parents.* This includes *fathers* as well as *mothers.* A lot of women have had guilt trips laid on them for working outside the home, but isn't it interesting that nobody asks fathers how they manage to balance fatherhood and a career? Some mothers have such great jobs that their husbands stay home with the kids, or the parents arrange their schedules to be available as co-caregivers. This is a viable option from the standpoint of your children's needs, especially for older children. There is no research that indicates that mothers are necessarily more effective greeters and caregivers for the assorted hurts and wounds of older children than fathers.

Another problem with working outside the home is that you will have to make painful choices to reconcile the demands of work and parenting. The same study of one thousand southern California families that found that eighty percent of working mothers would quit their jobs if they could, also found that fifty-eight percent of working mothers believed their parenting suffered because of the demands of their career. The same number believed their careers had suffered because of the demands of rearing children. You can do it, especially if you find creative ways of handling both your work and children, but it's tough. No matter how you look at it, it's not easy being a mother and a career woman—especially when your children are young. There are only twenty-four hours in a day and you need several of those to eat, sleep, rest, and take care of yourself.

THE FIRST THREE YEARS

Children especially need their mother's presence during the first three years of life. Your children's initial emotional attachment will be the most important one of their lives. During the first three years of life, infants and toddlers go through a God-created cycle of bonding with their mother and then gradually separate emotionally. They are like boats tied up to a dock, loading up on emotional fuel and supplies for three years before they are ready to leave the harbor. And they are like cars with small emotional fuel tanks that need to be regularly filled up with Mom's love in order to gradually learn that they can drive a little further between pit stops. If Mother isn't available, they are much more likely to feel needy and dependent because their emotional fuel tanks aren't full. Or they become so prematurely independent of Mother's love that they have trouble trusting others and being emotionally intimate in later life. They've learned too well how to get along without needing others.

For the past thirty years, psychologist Jay Belsky of Pennsylvania State University has studied the children of working mothers.[2] After carefully reviewing all of the relevant research as well as conducting studies of his own, Dr. Belsky concluded that babies who spend more than twenty hours a week in nonmaternal care during their first year of life risk having an insecure attachment to their mothers. They are also more likely to be noncompliant and aggressive in later childhood than children who spend less time in day care. Dr. Belsky is quick to point out that putting infants in a day care center does not invariably cause problems; some children do fine. The type of care, the type of child, and the type of parent all influence the outcome. But there is a very substantial body of literature that associates extensive nonmaternal care with higher levels of disobedience and aggression in the toddler through elementary school years.

Dr. Belsky's research tells us what most of us have known intuitively all along—children need their parents. Because of the potentially serious consequences of a mother working during these earliest years of life, I never recommend it unless there is no other reasonable way for the family to function. Even a steady babysitter or a grandparent cannot fully replace Mom during these earliest months and years of life. If you must work, don't lay a guilt trip on yourself—your children can still do fine. But if you have a choice, do yourself and your children a favor and don't go back to work until they are at least three years of age.

DAY CARE DAYS

By the time children reach three or four, they are generally ready for new experiences like day care centers, nursery schools, and daytime babysitters. I'm not saying these arrangements are ideal, and that every child should have them—I think it's great if mothers don't have to work and if they can be their children's primary caregivers throughout their preschool days and even longer. But I am also saying that by the time your children are three years old, they should have developed a pretty solid memory of their secure and lasting attachment to you that they will carry with them in their minds even when you are away. By far, many children can handle separations if they are necessary.

EACH CHILD IS DIFFERENT

After children reach three or four years of age, they vary greatly in their need for Mother. Some children are very independent and can cope well with two working parents. Others have great difficulty adapting to having their mothers work—even as late as the adolescent years. When our daughter, Debbie, was a middle adolescent, she encouraged her mom to work part-time. Debbie knew that her mom would enjoy a job, and that we could use some extra money for her and her brother's college education, and Debbie herself was emotionally ready for a little more space. She had been close to her mom for fifteen years and, as a fifteen-year-old, she was ready to be more independent. Once Kathy took the job, Debbie was proud that her mom was using abilities she hadn't been able to exercise as a homemaker. I'm also sure Debbie was encouraged to realize that she, too, had the ability to step into the work force when she grew up.

Other teenagers feel just the opposite. During a seminar for parents a few weeks ago, I asked the participants to write me a letter on the topic, "If I had it to do over again." One of those letters shed a lot of light on the struggles of being a working mom.

At one point in time, three of my children were in their teens. It was at this stage that I decided to go to work so I could bring in more income for my children's education. My intentions were sincere, and I was looking out for their good. However, I realize now that it caused me to fall short in other areas.

No longer was I available when they came home from school. We used to sit and share the good and bad things that happened that day. Nor was I able to spend one-on-one time with each of them. Nor was I able to observe the changes or moods that were taking place.

As a result of my working full-time and having many of the normal household routines to accomplish when I was home—plus meeting my husband's needs—I slowly pushed my children away from the intimacy we once shared. They no longer felt comfortable taking up my time. They began to alienate themselves.

I believe now that God would have had me remain in the home, nurturing and building into each one of my children's lives. It's possible I could have helped with the income some way from our home. Or perhaps I could have trusted God to provide when the time arose—as in fact he did! I see now how important a secure and loving home is when children are going through the many changes of adolescence. They need a refuge and parents who are modeling God's love and patience during those years.

As I read this letter I thought, *This is a very sensitive parent. She is able to look back and see some of the things her children missed and realize there were other options.* Then I looked at the closing. It read, "Love in Christ, Kryslie, the daughter of this mother."

The letter was not written by a parent. It was written by a teenage daughter who had had a very good relationship with her mother. But once her mom started working, there was less time to communicate with each other, and Kryslie felt pushed aside. Even though her mother was working to help pay for Kryslie's college education, she wished her mom would have stayed at home.

Not all teenagers feel this way. Some children are ready for their moms to go to work from the time they enter preschool. But others need their mother's full-time emotional support all the way through high school.

DON'T FORGET YOUR OWN NEEDS

Finally, remember that you have a responsibility to yourself as well as for your children. Although it might be nice if all mothers took to parenting like ducks to water and found perfect fulfillment in being twenty-four-hour parents, many don't. You may need a change of pace and the extra intellectual stimulation of interacting with adults and finding fulfillment by exercising your talents in the workplace. You may actually be a better mother when you *don't* spend eighteen hours a day with a two-year-old.

I have a friend who found fulfillment in the workplace as a choice of her own, not out of necessity. She began selling real estate in her early forties. Her children were in high school, her husband had a good job, and she wanted a new challenge. She could have kept chasing after her kids' school activities or thrown herself into church work or a round of social activities, but she really wanted to try a full-time job. Now she enjoys her career immensely and is quite successful.

Her conservative, elderly father, however, just cannot understand why she has gone back to work. He keeps reminding her that she doesn't need the money, and that a woman's place is in the home. No matter how my friend tries to explain herself, her father just can't comprehend the fact that she *enjoys* working. She is not running from anything. She is not escaping. She is not a frustrated person. She just enjoys meeting people, showing homes, working out contracts, and challenging herself. And now that her children have left the nest, she has a smaller void in her life than many mothers.

GO ON WITHOUT GUILT

If you decide it's best for you to work, be prepared for a lot of intense feelings. The stress of rearing children while you are holding down a job is obvious. So is the potential for marital conflicts caused by having to reallocate household duties and work out babysitting, day care, and transportation. But watch out for another emotional reaction—guilt. There probably isn't a working mother in America who doesn't feel guilty about leaving her children in a day care center, or not being home to greet her children when they return from school. There will be a little tension and at least a few struggles over leaving your children in someone else's care. But be careful—if you have thoughtfully considered your children's needs as well as your own, and you have decided it is best to work, don't let guilt ruin your life.

Doonesbury   BY GARRY TRUDEAU

Although I strongly believe that children need their mothers, let's be realistic. Many mothers have to work and you probably considered all of the pros and cons very carefully before you started. If you did, then try to move ahead without guilt. Remember that it isn't just the quantity of time, quality counts, too—as long as you don't use that as an excuse to neglect your children's needs. A couple of good hours with your children can beat a dozen hours of conflict. A lot of working mothers have reared wonderful, healthy, and happy children.

NOW THAT YOU ARE WORKING

If you have taken the plunge into the world of work, you have probably already found ways to conserve your energy and tactics for delegating work. Here are a few other tips to stimulate your thinking.

The starting place for a good experience as a working mom is to *recognize your limits*. Let's face it, you simply cannot hold down a full-time job and be a full-time mother. There are only twenty-four hours in a day. And time is not the only issue. There is physical and emotional fatigue. If you work days, you won't come home bursting with energy, excited over the prospect of tackling household chores, settling squabbles, soothing hurt feelings, and playing with your children.

Unless you want to push yourself to the brink of insanity, you must set realistic expectations for yourself at home and work. Some mothers do this by limiting themselves to part-time positions. Others work at home or rearrange their work hours to match the times they need to pick up children. Others get help from their spouse or simply agree to let some things go undone. Don't feel like you have to fix a four-course meal every night, have the house spotless, and spend lengthy, uninterrupted time with your children daily. It's just not humanly possible.

One single working mother put it this way: "There are some concessions I have had to make. I have become 'comfortably uncomfortable' with a certain level of messiness around the house. I close all the bedroom doors when company comes and give my kids strict orders not to open them. Since I don't have a dishwasher, we eat the things that I thaw or heat almost exclusively on paper plates to save time. If I entertain, it's always informal and everyone brings something. Gone are the days of sit-down dinners."

You will have to decide for yourself what things are absolutely essential, and you will have to let some things go. This poem gives a nice perspective:

Cleaning and dusting can wait till tomorrow,
For babies grow up, we've learned to our sorrow.
So fly away cobwebs, and dust go to sleep.
I'm rocking my baby, and babies don't keep!

Get Help

When I asked Patti, the single mother of three children, the one thing that helped her survive a demanding job and caring for her children, she immediately answered, "My live-in." Patti found a young girl who needed work and a place to stay, and she was able to hire her for slightly less money than she had been paying for a babysitter to take care of her infant son and day care for her two older children.

A live-in can be expensive, and it doesn't make sense to pay most of your salary to hire one. But in Patti's situation, it was actually cheaper. And her live-in doesn't just babysit. She helps with the housework and the cooking, and the kids love her. It wasn't easy finding a good live-in. Patti tried three other young women who didn't work out before she found a great one. But once she did, her life and the lives of her children improved by leaps and bounds.

Another way to survive (and maybe even thrive!) is to enlist the help of family members. If you are married, don't let your husband get by thinking that you will work full-time and still handle all of the household chores. I grew up on a farm where there was a pretty clear division between men's work and women's work. But when our son and daughter reached late and middle adolescence and my wife went back to work, I decided to do my part. Since that time, I have done my share of laundry, ironed my own shirts, cooked half of our meals, and done most of our grocery shopping. It wouldn't be fair to Kathy to expect her to handle all those responsibilities, the rest of the household chores, and a full-time job.

Sometimes relatives can help. One single mother told me, "The saving thing for me has been my mother and my sister. Between the two of them I don't think I've paid for a babysitter ten times. I don't know what I would do without their help." And don't forget your children. If your children are old enough to do some work around the house, see that they do their share. It is amazing what it means to come home at the end of the day and see the house in order and dinner on the stove! Besides that, your children need to learn to work. Finally, if your husband and children can't help you out, and you can't afford a live-in, perhaps you can pay someone to come in once or twice a month for the heavy cleaning. It may cost you, but it isn't realistic to try to do everything by yourself.

Find Creative Solutions

Now that so many women are working, businesses are a lot more sensitive to the needs of working mothers. Job sharing, an almost unheard-of practice thirty years ago, is increasingly common. Joan, one of our closest neighbors, was able to work out a job sharing arrangement in the public school district where she teaches. She and another mother each put in two and a half days a week and were even able to keep their fringe benefits when their children were young. Half-time jobs with reduced benefits are sometimes available. And don't forget the possibility of working at home or telecommuting. With a computer and a modem, many men and women are carrying out a significant portion of their work from home.

I recently found a great book I recommend to working mothers. It's called *The Best Jobs in America for Parents Who Want Careers and Time for Children Too.*[3] In a realistic manner, the authors discuss how to find or create a flexible job that will help you make time to be a loving parent while also working. They discuss changes in the workplace like job sharing, on-site child care, flexible hours, unpaid leaves, shortened work weeks, and telecommuting. They even list twenty-five American companies that have the most progressive and flexible work policies for women. They don't deal with the emotional or spiritual questions of working mothers, but they have a wealth of insight into practical ways of finding or creating work situations that will enable you to do the best job possible with your children as well as your work.

In case you think flexible jobs are impossible to come by, read this encouraging story of Jean, a single mother of two:

> I didn't want to work while my kids were young, but I had to. My employer is sensitive to my needs and lets me have an hour and a half for lunch each day so I can take my kids to the park. He is also understanding about things like doctor's visits. I go in early to make up the hours, but as long as I get my work done, he remains flexible.

Not all companies are this accommodating, but don't settle for a rigid eight-to-five job if you can find a more flexible one.

Make Time for Yourself

As important as your children are, they aren't the entire story. Don't neglect your own needs. You need time for refreshing and renewing. This is easier said than done, but you must find time to be alone. If you are married, spend time with your husband and other couples, or leave the children with your husband so you can have some time with your friends. This will be more difficult if you are single, but you've got to do it if you are going to survive. Gloria, a single mom, runs three miles six days a week. She told me, "It gives me a half hour without anything else coming into my head. I need that quiet time to think and plan. Sometimes my kids get tired of my running, but it's an absolute necessity for me. Sometimes they go to the track with me."

Nancy told me, "My kids know that the first thirty minutes when I get home from work are mine. I have to take my shoes off, unwind, and go through the mail. I make it clear that it isn't about them. It's about me and my day. After I've done that, I'm ready to be a mom again. If I don't give myself that time, I'm a big grouch."

Gloria and Nancy weren't being selfish. Even Jesus needed time away from his disciples to be alone. You will be able to handle your other responsibilities with greater confidence and strength when you take some renewal time for yourself.

SOME ADVICE ESPECIALLY FOR SOLO PARENTS

It's hard enough to be a married working mother, but being a single working mom is a herculean task. Unless you have a roommate, you have no one to share the household chores, no adult to come home to talk to, no one to help with the finances, and no one to help with the children.

The principles we have discussed in this chapter, and throughout the book, apply to the single parent household, but some will be more difficult to implement. For example, it's harder to take time for yourself when you don't have a spouse to watch the children. It's also difficult to choose between priorities when you have to do everything anyway. And you may not have the option of a part-time job, if you can't live on the income it produces. At the same time, it may be even more important to apply some of the suggestions in this chapter. For example, it's critical to keep up a decent social life in order to avoid isolation.

You didn't become a solo mother without some kind of tragedy, whether it was the death of your mate, a divorce, or a pregnancy outside of marriage. These tragedies can create intense feelings of grief, loss, guilt, or shame, and it's easy to withdraw from friends and family because you feel embarrassed or different. But isolation only makes things more tough. As one single mother put it, "When you don't have money to cover the utility bills, the baby won't shut up, and the toddler just spilled juice on the rug, you'd better have the phone number of at least one friend, for your sanity and your children's safety."

Along with supportive friends, it also helps to keep a clear perspective. Solo parenting is difficult, and if you only focus on your frantic schedule, limited finances, or the impact an absent father might make on your children, it can really get you down. But that isn't the entire picture. Several years ago I led a weekend workshop for solo parents. During our discussions, I began to realize how many false assumptions there were about single parents. I asked the conferees to make a list of the concerns they had about single parenting. Then, we discussed whether they were true.

We realized that things often aren't as bad as we may fear. For example, one solo parent mentioned the old adage, "Two parents are better than one." But we all agreed that one good parent is usually better than two lousy ones—or two parents in constant conflict. Someone else mentioned the belief that children from one-parent homes usually grow up with serious problems. We soon agreed that all children grow up with some emotional wounds, and that solo parents can rear healthy children.

Someone mentioned the belief that, after divorce, life's problems increase. Many heartily agreed when someone reminded her that after divorce, at least one of life's biggest problems may be gone! Divorce or loss of a mate through death is painful—and it does bring problems. But singleness can be preferable to an abusive, lousy marriage.

Another member said she kept hearing it was impossible for solo parents to raise children with good sexual adjustment. Of course, it's harder for one parent to help her children develop healthy attitudes toward both sexes, but it's possible. There are male teachers at school and church and male role models at a lot of clubs and social activities, not to mention uncles, grandfathers, neighbors, and other male friends. Find ways to have your children spend more time with them.

These are just a few of the myths we discussed, but I think you see my point. Single parenting is difficult, but it is not all bad, and it is not impossible. If you think creatively and learn to take care of yourself as well as your children, you can do a great job and have wonderful experiences with your children. Chances are, you will look back and be amazed at the challenges you handled, the strength you developed, and the growth you experienced by persevering on a daily basis.

There is another thing I've learned from single mothers. At first it absolutely shocked me, but as I have thought about it, I realize that it makes a lot of sense. Without exception, the single mothers I know who are coping well are all involved in some form of ministry or outreach beyond their own family. The first time a single mom told me she gave two evenings a month to work with abused children, I couldn't imagine how she found the time. With her frantic schedule, I assumed that she would grab every free minute for herself and her children. But Julie told me, "Oh, no. I need to give to someone else, and when I do, I get back even more." As I talked with other single moms, I heard the same thing over and over. One mom told me, "My son and I spend Christmas Eve together, since he is with his father on Christmas Day. The past four years I have gone to the inner city to serve Christmas lunch to the homeless. This year my girlfriend went with me. She is an artist and went from table to table drawing caricatures. There were enough servers, so I played with the kids, visited with people, and prayed silently. Then we delivered meals to several homebound people. By the time we got home and put our turkey in the oven it was 5:15 P.M. We watched a video and had a candlelight dinner at 9:00 that night. It tasted as good as any Christmas dinner ever did. I really had a great day."

I don't fully understand how single working mothers can do everything they do for their own families and still reach out to others. But for the single moms I know, giving seems to be as important for them as it is for those to whom they give. They tell me they always get back more than they give, and that they realize how blessed they are when they see others in even more serious circumstances.

Building a Home that Lasts

The last thing that I would like to share with single parents—and all parents for that matter—is this:

Unless the Lord builds the house,
   its builders labor in vain.
Unless the Lord watches over the city,
   the watchmen stand guard in vain.
In vain you rise early
   and stay up late,
toiling for food to eat—
   for he grants sleep to those he loves.[4]

Isn't this a great truth? The Lord knows you rise early, stay up late, and toil for food. He knows you're working hard, and he reminds you that you are not alone. He is building your house with you.

Jackie, who wrote me the letter about choosing not to work full-time and not to put her son in day care, told me, "I can tolerate hard work as long as I believe it will accomplish something, but the thought of laboring hard and having it be in vain is almost unbearable to me. Every morning I get up and ask God to build my house and my son's house. I extend myself as much as I can, but in the end I trust Calvin to the Lord. I trust God to cover my mistakes and inadequacies as a parent. No mother can do it all. We have to trust our children to the Lord!"

I wholeheartedly agree. In those tough times, when it feels like there is no way you can do it all, you can know that God is working, too. Sometimes he provides in tangible ways like a friend who offers urgently-needed help to fix the plumbing, mow the yard, or paint the house. Sometimes he provides with unexpected income or a babysitter. Sometimes he provides friendships with people who know how hard single parenting is. And sometimes his quiet help is behind the scenes, gently loving you and assuring you that your work is not in vain.

RECAP

Decisions about working while you are rearing children should include consideration of the needs of your entire family. If you don't work outside the home, you may occasionally feel burdened by your parental duties and yearn for some extra money, or the opportunity to express yourself in the workplace. If you decide to take a job, you will have a harder time meeting the needs of your children, and you may encounter a lot of physical and emotional fatigue. But if you must work, or if you decide that is best for you and your family, be sure to think and plan carefully. There are creative options and ways of coping with the challenges of being a mother and an employee if you take the time to find them.

Notes

1. For a realistic discussion of how much you may actually make after all expenses, see "Can you afford to Quit?" *Parents Magazine*, August 1990, 74–79, 168–69.

2. Jay Belsky, "Developmental risks associated with infant day care: attachment, insecurity, noncompliance, and aggression." S. M. Chehrazi (ed.), *Balancing Working and Parenting: Psychological and Developmental Implications of Day Care* (New York: American Psychiatric Press, forthcoming).

3. S. B. Dynerman and L. O. Hayes, *The Best Jobs in America for Parents Who Want Careers and Time for Children Too* (New York: Ballantine, 1991).

4. Psalms 127:1–2.

CHAPTER 14

Questions Parents Ask

For twenty years I have had the privilege of talking to parents throughout the United States and many other parts of the world. It's amazing how I hear the same questions from parents whether they live in Seattle, or St. Louis, or São Paulo, Brazil. In earlier chapters, I've answered many of the most common questions parents ask, but here are a few we haven't discussed yet—questions about children who lie, misbehave in public, constantly interrupt, fight with their siblings, or keep waking up in the middle of the night. In a "Dear Abby" format, here are the questions and my answers:

Dear Dr. Narramore:

I simply cannot bear hearing my child cry at night, so I get up five or six times. Can you help me? I am. . .

Sleepless in Seattle

Dear Sleepless,

Few experiences are more frustrating, more exhausting, and more dreaded than repeatedly dragging yourself out of bed in the middle of the night to calm a crying child. Parents who are going through this misery are easily identified by their slow pace, their haggard looks, and the dark circles beneath their eyes. If you greet them, they either gaze past you with a glassy stare or, at best, manage a nod of recognition. But behind their sleepy exteriors they are asking, *Isn't there something I can do?*

Yes, there is. In fact there are two things to be done. If your child is less than a year of age, you can comfort yourself by knowing that it won't last forever, even though it is currently driving you insane. Unfortunately, that's about all you can do. Since infants don't have the capacity to tolerate fear, sadness, and physical distress without their mom or dad, you are going to have to respond to their nighttime crying just as you do in the day: temporarily stop what you are doing—even sleep—to pick them up and calm them. I know that's incredibly tough, but you have to remind yourself that taking care of a crying baby is one of the "joys" of parenting that soon will pass. An infant's cries are not an expression of sinful egoism that needs to be extinguished. Crying is an expression of some fear or physical discomfort. Infants cry because that is their only way of telling you their needs and because they aren't able to comfort themselves yet.

Fortunately, by the time your babies turn into toddlers, certainly by fourteen months of age, you can move beyond the first parental role which requires you to be on twenty-four-hour call. By that age your children will have matured enough to know you care for them even though you aren't always physically present. This allows you to apply the technique I'm about to describe. I can *almost* guarantee you that in about one week your child will be sleeping through the night.

This technique is built on three psychological facts. First, children have needs and you must do your part to meet them. Second, as children grow older they can increasingly tolerate not having all of their needs met immediately. Third, many behaviors can be extinguished by not rewarding them.

Here is how this technique works. First, the night you begin, let your child cry for a few minutes. It depends on your child, but three or four minutes is on the short side and ten minutes should be the longest. Don't let him cry longer, because he will panic or become so hysterical he won't even remember why he started crying. This is too terrifying for a baby.

Second, at the end of five or ten minutes of crying, but before your child reaches the panic point, go to his room, pick him up and hug him until he quiets down, then tell him you love him, put him back in bed, and leave the room. Don't hold him until he goes back to sleep, because he will start expecting that every time. Just stay long enough to quiet his crying and then leave. You have quieted him enough when his crying turns to sniffling. This accomplishes two things. It lets your child know you care for him, but it also tells him you are not going to be with him as long as he might like. To put this another way, you have met his God-given need for parental love and care, but you are extinguishing his desire to always have you present precisely when and how he wants you.

The first two or three nights you apply this new routine, your child will begin crying again shortly after you put him back in bed. Then you apply the third step: Let him cry five minutes longer than you did the previous time, then go into his room and repeat the procedure. Each time he resumes crying, wait five minutes longer before you go into his room to calm him. This builds up the length of time he can go without you, while it keeps him from becoming too frightened or feeling completely abandoned.

Anytime your child wakes, simply repeat the procedure, beginning with an initial five- to ten-minute crying period. Go to his room to calm him, then lengthen the crying period before you attend to him again. This technique nearly always works within a few nights.

Before you begin this technique, be sure to get a grip on your guilt. It's hard to let a child cry, and you will probably feel miserably cruel the first couple of nights. But remember, you are meeting your child's God-given need and are not rewarding an excessive desire to have you present. By the time your child is fourteen months of age she can handle this as long as you attend to her lovingly within this framework.

Dear Dr. Narramore:

I can't get a straight answer out of little William. He lies about everything. He was playing with matches the other day and burned up my clothes basket full of clean clothes. Told me the dog did it.

Signed,
Liar, Liar, Pants on Fire

Dear Pants on Fire,

Scenes like yours happen in every home. Whether they are major deceptions, like stealing and outright lies, or "little things," like undone chores or broken curfew, every child occasionally hides the truth. The starting place for dealing with dishonesty is recognizing the reason your child is lying. A four-year-old who claims, "Daddy, I outran every child in school today," a six-year-old who claims he didn't break his mother's most precious vase, and a teenager who misses curfew and says his car ran out of gas, are probably distorting the truth for different reasons.

Young children have a natural tendency to exaggerate. They enjoy fairy tales and sometimes construct their own or embellish reality with fantasy. A little of this shouldn't alarm you. In fact, mature creativity springs from the soil of a good imagination. But some children do more than exaggerate a little. They embellish their achievements and stretch reality to gain attention or compensate for feeling inferior or inadequate. These children are telling us, "I don't like myself the way I am, so I have to make you think I'm different."

Let's say that your five-year-old runs into the house and proudly announces, "I outran every child in school today!" Don't agree or disagree until you have more information. You might say "Really! Tell me about it." If you still have doubts after he repeats his story, you might say, "*Every* child in school?" At this point most children will acknowledge it's really just the children in their class or the children they raced that day. But some persist, undaunted. If that happens you might reply, "You sure *are* a good runner and it would be great to outrun *all* the kids at school. But I'm not sure you can really outrun all the sixth-graders, too. They are pretty fast you know!" This way you avoid labeling your child a liar and protect his self-esteem, while still letting him know you want the truth.

Other children lie to avoid being punished. Like a six-year-old who breaks his mother's vase, they lie so they won't be caught. When my own children were young and I asked them, "Why do children lie?" they immediately answered, "To get out of trouble!" You can see how lying can easily be rewarded. When a child lies to avoid punishment and isn't caught, his lying is rewarded.

Just as some children lie to get *out* of trouble, others lie to get their brothers or sisters *in* trouble. Younger children are masters at stirring up conflict with older brothers or sisters, taking the "innocent" role, and getting their older siblings in trouble. I learned early on that when Richard seemed to be picking on his innocent little sister, Debbie wasn't always quite so innocent.

I asked Debbie, "What were *you* doing just before Richard walked into your room and hit you?"

"Nothing," she sweetly replied.

"You mean you were in your room playing with your Barbie dolls, and Richard just came in and hit you for no reason?" I asked.

"Nooo," she reluctantly (but *very* cutely) admitted. And upon further questioning, she would admit to going into Richard's room or making a face at him.

So be careful. Sometimes your "innocent" child will enhance the truth to get his or her more blatantly disobedient sibling into trouble.

For deceitful (instead of exaggerating) lies, bring the problem directly to your child's attention rather than trying to trap him further. Some parents have a habit of trying to "convict" their children like a sly prosecuting attorney. Knowing full well the late arrival of their teenage daughter, they innocently ask, "What time did you get in last night, honey?" Or, already knowing who the guilty party is, they say "Joey, do you know what happened to the money on the table?"

Questions like these are invitations to dishonesty. They set children up for a dishonest answer and imply that we don't know what happened when we really do. We are actually resorting to our own form of dishonesty by faking ignorance of the situation. This sets a poor example for our children. It is much better to simply say, "Joey, I saw the money in your room" or "Honey, you were out quite late last night." Statements like this, offered in a factual rather than an accusatory manner, give children the opportunity to tell the truth, even if it is belated.

Once you have calmly brought the problem to your child's attention, encourage him to tell you just what happened. Without condemning or pressuring, let him know you are concerned and would like to know what happened. Most children, of course, are afraid to tell the story truthfully. But if you let them know you aren't going to lose your temper or punish them in anger, they will probably open up. You might say something like, "Son, I realize we all have a tendency to hide the truth, but in the end it works out better not to lie. If you are afraid that I will be angry with you or punish you in anger, I want you to know I won't. I may have to discipline you to help you do better next time, but I will not be angry at you for telling me the truth. It's very important for us to be honest with each other."

Once he tells the truth, let him know you understand why he was afraid to be honest with you. Offer him the same understanding you would like if you had been dishonest. This opens pathways of communication and makes honesty easier in the future. If you think he needs more discipline than he can receive from your talk, set a meaningful consequence that will remind him to think twice the next time.

Probably the most confusing lies are the repeated, gross untruths given out by pathological liars. Fortunately, this is rare, but a few children seem to have lost sight of either the realities of the world or their own moral sensibilities. Even when caught in blatant distortions, they refuse to admit their dishonesty. These children are likely to get involved in delinquent acts and are in need of professional help, since pathological lying can reflect a severe mental or emotional problem.

Finally, bring in biblical principles. Your children need to know that God sets a high priority on honesty, but don't use the Bible as a club to try to shame or condemn them. Hold out God's standards in an attitude of grace that models his acceptance and love for us. Just as God forgives you, your children need to know that you forgive them when they admit a mistake. Your forgiveness will give them freedom to be more honest next time, because they won't be so afraid.

To summarize, if our children are afraid of us—and especially if they are afraid we will angrily punish them when they make a mistake—they are more likely to lie or do whatever it takes to avoid our wrath. When children feel secure in our love and know that we are gracious and forgiving, they find it a lot easier to be honest—even if that means facing discipline that is lovingly administered.

Dear Dr. Narramore:

Whenever I go grocery shopping with the quints (Larry, Gary, Mary, Sherry, and Terry) things seem to get out of hand. I won't give details, but last week there was an accident involving three of the quints, the live lobster display, five pounds of ground beef, some-

one's seeing-eye dog, and the entire feminine hygiene aisle. We have been banned from nearly every grocery store in town. What do you suggest?

Famished in Fargo

Dear Famished,

In chapter 5, I suggested that the best way to handle temper tantrums at home is to ignore them. Once children realize they aren't going to get attention or control you with a tantrum, they usually stop. But what about acting up in public? You can't walk blithely down Aisle 5 of your local supermarket as your son is screaming at

"UHH..EXCUSE ME MA'AM, BUT YOU'VE...UH..TAKEN MY CART BY MISTAKE. I BELIEVE THAT'S YOURS OVER THERE."

the top of his lungs and rolling cans of fruit and vegetables down Aisle 3! So how can you handle acting up in public?

Let's say you have taken your preschooler to the local supermarket. Shortly after you enter the store, he disappears into the next aisle. Afraid of what he will do, you track him down and tell him to stay with you. A couple of minutes later he is pulling a can of aftershave off the shelf. Then he is asking if he can have some candy or his favorite drink. Then he starts whining, "I'm tired" or "Can we go home now?" Before long, he is crying, screaming, or into other trouble. What is going on in your child's mind that makes him create such a disturbance?

Imagine how you would feel if you entered a store with your mom. She is three times your size and starts down the aisle putting everything she wants in a gigantic (from your perspective) cart. Every time you see something you want and try to put it in the cart, your mother tells you to put it back. Up and down the aisles you go. Every goodie your parent wants, she gets. Everything you want goes back on the shelf. After awhile this gets old. It's boring and frustrating. So how can you get even with the giant, force her to cut the trip short, or get something you would like? The obvious answer: Throw a tantrum or make a fuss. One mother told me her frustrated son sat sullenly in the cart through her entire shopping trip. Then just as she was next in line at the check-out counter, he stood up and yelled at the top of his voice, "Help! Help! This woman's not my mother." Fortunately, the manager knew her, so she wasn't carted off to jail. But her son had gotten his revenge!

Here's how to handle this problem. First, don't take your children into a situation you know will drive them crazy unless it's absolutely necessary. If you can't leave them with someone, be prepared to keep them busy in the market. Bring a toy along, or if they are old enough, let them get a few items off the shelf for you—not eggs or other breakables, but try to keep them busy. You might also promise them a reward of candy or gum on the way out. If they still act up, take them away from other shoppers and come up with a good consequence. If they are old enough and it is safe, make them sit in a corner of the store. If they are older children, and it is safe, let them stay in the car. If not, make them stay in the cart, lose their reward at the checkout stand, or stay home next time. But before you go to these corrective measures, remember the real problem. They are bored stiff and resentful that you get absolutely everything you want while they have nothing to occupy them. Your best solution is to solve the underlying problem.

Dear Dr. Narramore:

I can't talk on the phone for two minutes before my son starts whining for attention. I can't even have a cup of coffee with my neighbor. Help!

Interrupted in Indiana

Dear Interrupted,

When your son starts whining the minute you get on the phone, you have three options. First, you can drop everything each time he calls. This will meet his immediate demand, give you temporary peace, and perhaps relieve your guilt for "neglecting" your child. But it won't solve the problem. In fact, since you have rewarded his cries with attention, it will increase the likelihood he will whine the next time he wants attention.

Another way to manage an excessive demand for attention is to ignore it. Simply refuse to listen and go on with your business. When your son finds out his interruptions aren't working, he might stop. But this creates another problem. What if he genuinely is feeling lonely and needs your love right now? We shouldn't ignore our children's desires for attention if they reflect a God-given need for love.

Your best option is to realize there is a difference between needing legitimate love and just wanting to be the center of things. You can tell the difference by asking yourself a few questions. Have you spent some quality, focused time with your child today? Have you hugged him and shown him physical affection? Are you communicating well? Have you shown him how important he is to you? Has he spent some time with friends today? Does he have plenty of interesting things to keep him occupied while you are busy with your activities? Are you willing to drop some of your activities to spend time with him when he really needs it?

If you can answer yes to most of these questions, you can safely conclude your son probably isn't needing more love; he is demanding too much attention. Tell him something like this: "Rob, you know how much Mommy loves you and likes to be with you. We have had some good times today. Now I want to talk with my friend. When the clock gets to eleven we can play some more. But if you call again before eleven, I will not come and I will not answer. You can play with your toys while Mommy talks on the phone." By doing this, you assure your child of your love, but you refuse to let him ruin your day.

This works the same way for a child who interrupts when you are working or having coffee with a friend. Stop what you are doing once. Remind him of the time you've had together and when you will be together again. Offer a few suggestions for how he can occupy his time. But if he complains that he doesn't want to do those things, tell him, "I don't know what will interest you, honey, but I'm sure you can find something." Then go on with your conversation and don't let him interrupt again. If he does, put him in his room and tell him not to come out until he can stop interrupting. Don't use this technique as an excuse to ignore your child's need to be with you. If he is interrupting you a lot, that may be his way of telling you he needs more time with you. But if his needs are being met, protect your own time by not caving in to demands for instant gratification.

Dear Dr. Narramore:

My son Rocky keeps beating up on his siblings. No amount of punishment seems to help. What do you suggest?

Signed,
Mrs. Balboa

Dear Mrs. Balboa,

Think how it must feel to be the oldest child in a family. For one or more years you are the center of your parents' attention. Then a baby brother or sister arrives on the scene and starts taking a lot of your parents' time, energy, and love. You enjoy some things about your baby brother or sister, but you also feel a little pushed aside, left out, or worse yet—replaced. So how will you cope with this inexplicable intrusion into your perfect world? You might revert to baby talk, even though you have previously learned to speak maturely. Or you might lose bladder or bowel control in the hope of stealing back your mother's attention. But since these efforts may just bring criticism or scorn, and are temporary solutions, you have to find other ways to cope. If you can't think of any creative ways to get more attention from your mom and dad, the next best alternative is to get revenge on the newcomer. This is the most common cause of sibling fights. By teasing, poking, twisting, pinching, or hitting the intruder, you get back at your parents too. You tell your parents, "I'm hurt that you left me for another baby and I want to make him suffer." You also hope to teach the little intruder a lesson.

Or think how it feels to be the second child or the baby of the family. As soon as you are old enough to know what's going on, you notice that your older siblings are much better off than you. They can run faster, stay up later, and have more privileges. To top it off, they can beat you up! You feel like a second-class citizen, and it makes you angry. Beating up an older sibling is a great fantasy, but hard to execute. What you *can* do is tease them or provoke them until they hurt you. Then you can run crying to Mother and get them in trouble. It's a foolproof plan.

The mother of a thirteen-year-old boy and a ten-year-old girl asked if I thought her son might be seeking attention by continually picking on his little sister. I told her, "Definitely, but I also wonder what your girl is doing to provoke him." "Oh, nothing," the mom replied. "Katie is an angel."

Finding it hard to believe that any ten-year-old could be an angel, I replied, "Come on, now. She can't be *that* perfect!" "No," the mother said. "She really is. She will be sitting right next to me on the couch and Vernon will come up and hit her for no reason." Seeing "innocent" Katie's strategy for attention, I asked the mother, "Why is your daughter sitting next to you?" She said, "Because we are very close."

There was dead silence in the room as something clicked in her mind. "Oh," the mother said. "Now I see it. Vernon is feeling left out and needs attention. Katie gets it by being good, so Vernon gets it by picking on her."

As we continued talking, the mother saw through more of her daughter's "innocent" behavior. When Vernon upset their mother, Katie "maturely" told him, "Oh, leave Mother alone. You're such a stupid kid. Can't you see you're upsetting her?" The mother told me, "I used to think Katie was being such a good girl, and it was too bad Vernon wasn't behaving that way! Now I realize she was doing exactly what would antagonize a thirteen-year-old brother, and I was falling for it. Who needs a ten-year-old sister saying, "I'm closer to mother and you are stupid"?

These scenarios show why children fight. They are feeling left out, unimportant, or rejected. That makes them angry, so they start fighting to get revenge, attention, or to settle some other emotional score, like building up their confidence by proving they are stronger than their brother or sister. In others words, anytime your children feel unloved, unworthy, incompetent, or bored, they may turn to fighting as a substitute for their God-given needs or to get revenge on the one who makes them feel that way.

Once you know why your kids are fighting, you can take three steps to prevent it. First, do all you can to meet their underlying needs. If your oldest child is picking on his brother because he feels pushed aside, find ways to spend more time with him alone so you can meet his God-given need. If he is beating up on his brother to build up his confidence, get him on a soccer team or help him find something he is good at. Compliment him, praise him, and help him develop skills that will let him feel stronger and more competent.

Second, stop rewarding your children's fighting. If your youngest is pestering your oldest and then playing innocent when the oldest one evens the score, don't side with the young one and reward his efforts to get his brother in trouble. One of the best ways to handle fighting is to let them work things out themselves. In fact, when no adults are around, children usually work out their conflicts. If you have ever flattened yourself against a door and secretly listened to your children at play, you probably noticed that they get along relatively well. They are capable of playing together and working out misunderstandings. But the minute they know you are watching them, they start fighting. This is because when they are alone, they aren't vying for your attention and they know no one will intervene. Forced to get their attention from each other and settle their own squabbles, they decide to work them out themselves.

When our daughter was eighteen months and our son was four years old, I witnessed them working out a conflict. I was weeding in the yard while Debbie was in her playpen nearby. Richard came along with nothing better to do than pick a fight, and made the first move. He grabbed the beads Debbie was playing with. This sent Debbie into wails calculated to bring in parental reinforcements to her position. I didn't move. Richard got angry at Debbie's attempt to rat on him. He picked up my garden shovel (which had a five-foot handle) and said to Debbie, "I'm going to hit you." Then he headed toward her playpen, shovel in hand. My heart skipped a beat, and I almost jumped up to stop him, but then I asked myself, "What would

I tell another parent to do in the same situation?" I knew normal children wouldn't purposely inflict severe harm on others. I also knew Richard was trying to get a rise out of me, since he purposely threatened Debbie within my hearing. If he really wanted to clobber her with a shovel, he wouldn't have let me know about it!

I kept working as if I hadn't heard a word, slyly keeping one eye on Richard. I didn't trust him completely, and a garden shovel could make a big gash in my sweet little girl's pretty blond head! Richard advanced slowly, raised the shovel over Debbie's head, and said again, "I'm going to hit you." By now I was really worried, but I forced myself to stay out of their fight. Finally Richard turned the shovel around to the handle, lowered it toward Debbie and *very* gently touched her on the head. Just as I breathed a sigh of relief, little Debbie slapped Richard in the face! That ended it, and Richard retreated into the house. He really didn't want to injure his sister. He was just trying to get my attention. And Debbie proved beyond all doubt she could take care of herself—even at eighteen months!

This doesn't mean that older children cannot hurt younger ones, and occasionally they will. But unless children are severely emotionally disturbed, they won't seriously injure each other on purpose. If your children actually hurt each other, they will usually feel some remorse. I saw this in our own children, too. When Richard hurt Debbie, and we told him, "Tell her you're sorry," he responded with a superficial and almost sarcastic, "I'm sorry." But once when Richard didn't know I was nearby and he hurt his sister, I saw him take her in his arms and hug her and say a very genuine and heartfelt "I'm sorry, Debbie." This is true brotherly love, and it can be learned only when we stay out of our children's fights.

If you are convinced that one of your children will hurt the other one, here's an alternative. Sit down with your children and tell them you like to see them play together, but there is too much fighting. Ask them why they are fighting and settle any legitimate gripes like, "He comes into my room" or "He takes my things." You can solve these preliminary causes by setting up a logical consequence like, "If you take one of your sister's toys without asking, she can play with anything of yours she wants." Then, simply tell your children, "Next time you start arguing and fighting you will each have to go to your room for a half hour." That should do it. But if it doesn't, add ten minutes to the time-out each time. The combination of addressing the cause and setting up a logical consequence of time will make a big dent in your children's fighting.

One final thing. When you are trying to teach your children not to fight, don't forget the most important thing: modeling. The best way to teach your children how to get along is to set a good example. If you can calmly talk things over and find a solution when you have a conflict with your mate, your friend, or your children, they will be more likely to follow your example.

RECAP

Like the rest of your children's behavior problems, difficulty sleeping, telling the truth, acting up in public, interrupting, and fighting can be handled by following a few simple steps. First, figure out why they are misbehaving. Second, try to solve that problem by meeting their underlying God-given need (boredom, lack of attention, fear, resentment, etc.). Third, remove any rewards your children are getting for their misbehavior and start rewarding their positive behavior. Finally, after you have done all you can to solve the underlying problem, institute some form of corrective discipline. The specific discipline will vary from time to time, but these steps apply to every misbehavior.

CHAPTER 15

Keeping Ahead of Your Children

There is a story told about a man named Dave who loved children. He was an older gentleman, always relaxed and patient with the neighborhood kids, and happy to have them hang out at his house. One day Dave poured a new cement driveway, and in the stealth of night some mischievous children found his fresh cement. They put their footprints and initials all over Dave's new driveway. The next morning when he discovered the results, Dave blew his stack. His loud threats echoed between the neighborhood houses. It was clear to everyone he wanted to throttle the culprits.

One of the neighbors was surprised by Dave's outburst because it seemed so out of character. When he got up the nerve to ask Dave about his sudden change of attitude he said, "Dave, you're usually so mellow. Why are you so angry all of a sudden? I thought you loved children." Dave thought awhile and then replied, "I love them in the abstract, but not in the concrete!"

The moral of this story applies to this book. It is one thing to read some abstract theory; it is another matter to make concrete applications in your own family. When you put this book down, you may walk away with some good ideas and a better understanding of your children and their needs. You may even apply a few of the training tools. But unless you decide to make some concrete changes, you won't see much difference in your children or in your parenting style. It doesn't help a bit to understand how rewards and natural and logical consequences work if you don't put them into practice. It does not help to know children need to be disciplined in love unless you learn to manage your anger. And it's not enough to know how fragile a young child's self-esteem can be unless you start doing something to help him feel better about himself.

Josh was a laid-back fourteen-year-old who had been bringing home Ds since junior high. Keith and Julie tried everything they knew to get him to bring up his grades. They nagged him. They warned that he wouldn't get into college. They bribed him, and they shamed him—all to no avail. After I shared the principle of natural consequences with them, I suggested that since none of their efforts were working, they might as well let Josh take responsibility for his own grades. At first they panicked. Julie said, "But he'll fail." "What's he doing now?" I asked. Then I pointed out that things couldn't get much worse, and that maybe Josh was actually doing poorly because of his parents' pressure. They were sure that couldn't be the case, but decided to give it a try.

The next evening they told Josh, "We are sorry we have been bugging you about your grades. School is really your responsibility. If you want to do better, that's fine, but if you choose to get Ds that is up to you." Next term Josh got all Cs! Since he was unconsciously failing in order to get back at his pressuring parents, once they laid off, he lost his reason to underachieve.

I don't recommend this solution for all school problems. Some children need help structuring their time. Others need some consequences at home like, "No homework, no television." But the point is that Josh's parents had to put some principles into practice before anything would change.

You *can* be a better parent. You *can* learn to control your temper. You *can* train your children to pick up after themselves and do their chores. And you *can* help your children take responsibility for their actions by using appropriate natural and logical consequences. But you won't, if you walk away from this book without a commitment to action.

I urge you to go back through this book one chapter at a time in order to cement these ways of working with your children in your mind so you can start applying them. The best way to do that is to set aside a regular study time with your mate or a few friends. You don't need an expert to lead you, just get a group of concerned parents together who are willing to spend a little time improving their parenting skills. Arrange to meet once or twice a month for a couple of hours and cover one or two chapters each time you meet. Covenant with each other to not only read the chapter, but to apply at least one specific concept or suggestion from that chapter to your children that week.

To help you do this, I've written a companion workbook, the *Help! I'm a Parent Handbook*, which helps you apply the principles I have outlined here to specific family situations. You may decide to use the *Handbook* in a morning mothers' club, an evening couple's group, or even an adult Sunday school class. If you decide to not use the *Handbook*, at least review each chapter of this book and start applying its concepts to specific needs or problems in your family.

© 1991 Bil Keane
Dist. by Cowles Synd., Inc.

"Of COURSE I'd like to be the
ideal mother. But I'm too busy
raising children."

A couple of other things I've learned as I've talked to thousands of parents over the years: Don't try to change everything at once, and don't try to solve your children's biggest problems first. Start with a small or medium-sized problem and wait to tackle the biggest ones until you and your children get the hang of it.

It also helps to explain your changes in disciplinary strategy to your children so they won't be shocked or confused and think you are being unfair. Don't suddenly tell your children, "If you are late to dinner, you can't eat" or "If you are late for the bus, I won't drive you to school." Take a few minutes to sit with your children and tell them how and why things are going to change. If your plan is met by loud protests, tell your children, "I know this may be hard the first few days, but I'm sure we can all get the hang of it." Then ask if they have any other questions and give them an answer if they do. If they still protest, tell them, "I know this is scary, but we have tried the other way and it's just not working. I'm not trying to make things harder for you. I'm doing something that is going to make life better for all of us in the long run." Then calmly but firmly stick to your guns.

Don't expect everything to change the minute you initiate a new routine. Some changes will come quickly and easily, but others take longer. It may be easy to let your son experience the simple natural consequence of being cold if he goes out without his coat and he may learn his lesson the first time. But it will be more difficult to stop punishing your children in anger if that has been your style. And a child with low self-esteem won't suddenly feel great about himself because you have stopped criticizing him and begun to compliment him. That change will come slowly.

Here is one final reminder: There are no perfect parents. Effective parents are sensitive *most* of the time. They are able to admit their problems *most* of the time. They are able to discipline in love *most* of the time. And they are *generally* able to get into their children's shoes and understand how they feel and think. But even the best of parents are occasionally unaware of their children's needs, or lose their tempers, or do or say something they regret later. What you do after you blow it is often more important than your mistakes. When your children see that you are willing to admit your mistakes and promise to try to do better next time, they can be quite forgiving.

Well, that brings us to the end. Your children are a precious gift from God, and I hope you love them and enjoy them and are blessed by them as much as I have loved and enjoyed and been blessed by mine.